FASHION'S BIOFABRICATION REVOLUTION

FASHION'S BIOFABRICATION REVOLUTION

AYESHA AHMAD

NEW DEGREE PRESS

COPYRIGHT © 2020 AYESHA AHMAD

All rights reserved.

FASHION'S BIOFABRICATION REVOLUTION

ISBN   978-1-63676-510-5   *Paperback*
        978-1-63676-033-9   *Kindle Ebook*
        978-1-63676-034-6   *Ebook*

To Ammi, my fashion icon

CONTENTS

INTRODUCTION

Imagine being able to use your afternoon tea to create a jacket. Sounds crazy, right? Well, that's exactly what Suzanne Lee did.[1] Suzanne Lee is a New York-based fashion designer who constantly experiments with new fashion techniques and technology. In one of her experiments, Lee created a "kombucha culture," a mix of tea, sugar, bacteria, and other microorganisms. She grew this culture in an empty bathtub, creating a material that she describes as "looking like human skin."[1]

What Lee pioneered is unimaginable for the everyday fashion enthusiast, as most designers would not think to use bacteria to create a material for fabric. While the idea of a bacteria jacket sounds like a cute fashion fad, it has the potential to change the way the current fashion industry is producing clothing. It may not have been included amongst this season's must-haves, but you definitely need one in your wardrobe if you are looking to stay ahead of the trends of the future.

---

1   Suzanne Lee, "Grow your own clothes," filmed February 2011 at TED2011 in Long Beach, CA, video, 06:25.

In today's fast fashion industry, it's easy to get caught up in buying the next big thing. Every season brings a new trend to follow and, naturally, a desire to keep up with these new trends. As a result, many companies are mass-producing clothes to appeal to their trendsetting consumers. While this may be allowing consumers to stay stylish, this fashion cycle is detrimental to the environment.

According to a report published by Quantis, the fashion industry's mass production of apparel has an increasingly negative impact on climate change. Between 2005 and 2016, the industry's impact on climate change rose to 35 percent and is projected to grow from 2020 to 2030. While these figures are a bit daunting, Lee's experiment allows for an alternative to this destructive production. Hello, bacteria jacket!

As a Bioinformatics major, I am intrigued by Biology, whether it be microbes or the anatomy of the human body; the subject never fails to pique my interest. Simultaneously, I am a fashion enthusiast. Growing up, my mom influenced my interest in fashion as she would take her clothes and modify them. Whether adding accents to her shirts, or completely redesigning a dress, my mom hoped to emulate the styles she saw while flipping through *Vogue* or on a model strutting down a catwalk.

My mom and I always watched the runway shows of our favorite designers together, such as Tory Burch and Tommy Hilfiger. She taught me how to sew (even though I am not very good) and how to express myself through what I wear. For me, fashion is a creative outlet through which I showcase my vibrant personality.

Fashion and Biology have been major influences in my life. Still, I did not consider their overlap until I went down a Google rabbit hole and started to research about bacteria and spider silk—how companies and fashion designers are using these resources to challenge the way we currently wear clothes. I am excited to see where Biology will take the fashion industry and how it will help to create more sustainable methods of apparel production. This book is for creatives, inventors, or anyone interested in exploring something new.

While the intersection of Biology and Fashion is relatively new territory, the exploration of their intersection creates endless possibilities for both the scientific and fashion communities. These two industries are so completely different, making it hard to believe they could complement each other. What would a scientist and fashion designer talk to each other about anyway? Apparently, a lot more than you would expect. Because these two fields are so unrelated, I believe that they have the potential to create something extraordinary together.

What I have found has inspired me about the future of fashion and how nature is poised to disrupt it.

PART 1

THE GHOST OF FASHION PAST, THE GHOST OF FASHION PRESENT, AND THE GHOST OF FASHION YET TO COME

What was the fashion industry like before, how has it changed, and where is it going? In this section, we will explore these three questions. In the indigenous practices of Native Americans, there is a responsibility toward nature. Textile and garment making both use the resources that nature provides. Natural resources fuel the production of clothing.

With colonization and the industrial revolution, a new source of fuel was introduced: fossil fuels. These shifted the focus from nature to production. Today's fashion industry is fueled by an entirely new craze: the desire to stay up to date on the trends of our favorite influencers. This leads to the production of tons of clothing, as well as the expansion and pollution of natural resources in the process.

The future of fashion lies with connecting back to nature. Biotechnology provides this future through biofabrication. With biofabrication, we have the potential to not only create more sustainable alternatives, but also meet the demands of today's production too.

CHAPTER 1

THE FAST FASHION INDUSTRY

Whenever I get a brand-new dress, or I manage to put together an amazing outfit, my first instinct is to take a picture for the 'gram. I know I'm not the only one that posts an #OOTD (Outfit of the Day) pic when the occasion arises. The only problem is that once I display the outfit on my insta page, you'll probably never find me wearing it again. Why? Well, those #OOTD posts will not be original if I don't have a new outfit to post every day. Does this sound familiar? The desire to be trendy has been ingrained in us and it fuels the fast fashion ideology of buy, consume, and dispose.

When I think about the fashion industry, a few things come to mind: new designer collections released during fashion week, my constant desire to keep up with the trends, and my next purchase. While my thoughts surrounding the industry capture the glamour and glitz of being 'fashionable' in today's terms, the behind-the-scenes processes are not that glamorous.

INFLUENCER CULTURE AND FAST FASHION

If we take a closer look, the process of creating our clothes is far from appealing. Designer Eileen Fisher acknowledges the negative impact of the industry. When accepting an environmental award from Riverkeeper, she said, "The clothing industry is the second largest polluter in the world...second only to oil."[2] This is a jarring statement that makes me wonder about the byproduct waste produced when making the clothes we wear. As the statistics illustrate, the fashion industry generates a lot of waste and uses a lot of resources.

Fast fashion is a significant contributor to our pollution problem. The fast fashion business model includes using cheap materials and labor to create new clothing pieces as quickly as possible. Fast fashion thrives for many reasons, namely because of social media trends. Fast fashion brands see influencers wearing an expensive designer dress and create a copy of that dress, ready to sell on their website in a matter of days, sometimes even hours. The Kardashian-Jenner clan, who has a massive following on every social media platform, is one group of influencers whose style fast fashion is quick to copy. After Kylie Jenner's twenty-first birthday party, Fashion Nova released a collection of knockoffs of each sister's outfit for sale on their website.[3] The original romper Kylie wore at the party costs $8000. The knockoff on Fashion Nova costs about $40.[4,5]

---

2   Daniella Castiel, "How Fashion Affects People and the Environment," *Sierra Club*, November 29, 2016.

3   Krystin Arneson, "Fashion Nova Already Knocked Off Looks From Kylie Jenner's Birthday Party," *Glamour*, August 11, 2018.

4   Alyssa Bailey, "Exclusive: How Kylie Jenner Helped Create Her $8,000 Custom LaBourjoisie Jumpsuit For Her 21st Birthday," *Elle*, August 10, 2018.

5   "Birthday Bash Sequin Romper," Fashion Nova, accessed May 4, 2020.

While it seems like fast fashion gives the average person a chance to recreate the looks of their favorite celebrities at an affordable price, it holds a greater cost: our environment. A lot of resources go into creating garments. A report published in 2017 titled the *Pulse of the Fashion Industry* indicates that, in 2015, the industry used 79 billion cubic meters of water; enough to fill 32 million Olympic swimming pools. This water use is predicted to increase to 50 percent by 2030.[6] That is a significant amount of water, making it hard to imagine that those already massive figures are continuing to increase.

THE FAST FASHION SUPPLY CHAIN AND CHILD LABOR

The laborers behind the production of these garments work in poor conditions, receive low pay, and are mostly children. A report published by UNICEF and *The Guardian* states that 170 million children are employed in the fashion industry.[7] Families in impoverished countries send their children to work in these factories with the promise of good pay and healthy working conditions. A report published by the Centre for Multinational Corporation and the India Committee of the Netherlands indicates that job recruiters in South India promise families that their daughters will receive good pay, three nutritious meals, and schooling if they work in spinning mills.

One young girl working in Jeyavishnu expresses that she dislikes working at the mill. The recruiter, despite assuring

---

6   *Pulse of the Fashion Industry* (Global Fashion Agenda and The Boston Consulting Group, 2017), 11.

7   Josephine Moulds, "Child Labour in the fashion supply chain," *The Guardian,* n.d.

her and her family that she would be able to continue her education, did not fulfill these promises. Instead, workers work 12 hours a day and, after a year of work, they must work night shifts as well.[8] Recruiters give these families and young girls hope for a better life but, instead, the children are separated from their families and are working endless shifts.

FAST FASHION'S ENVIRONMENTAL IMPACT

According to a 2016 article published in McKinsey and Company, from 2000 to 2014, the average consumer purchased 60 percent more clothing.[9] Production of clothing has also doubled. While this may seem like a promising statistic for fashion economies and businesses, consumers do not wear most of this clothing. According to the United Nations Environmental Program, 85 percent of textiles end up in landfills.[10] That's an overwhelming majority of our garments. Many of these garments are not even worn before they are thrown into the landfill.

Not only do a majority of these garments end up in landfills, but the materials from which they are made are also

---

8   Martje Theuws and Pauline Overeem, "Flawed Fabrics: The abuse of girls and women workers in the South Asian Textile Industry (Centre for Research on Multinational Corporations and the Indian Committee of the Netherlands)," 39.

9   Nathalie Remy, Eveline Speelman, and Steven Swartz, "Style that's sustainable: A new fast fashion formula," *McKinsey & Company*, October 20, 2016.

10   Irena Zubcevic, Simone Cipriani, Maria Beatriz Mello da Cunha, Michael Stanley-Jones, Karen Newman, Lillian Liu, and Niclas Sevenningsen, "Fashion and the SDGs: what role for the UN?" Program for the International Conference Center Geneva, Geneva Switzerland, March 2018.

harmful to the environment. According to an article published by *Vox*, 60 percent of the fibers that make up garments—like polyester, nylon, and acrylic—are forms of plastic.[11] This plastic contributes to microplastic pollution in the ocean. According to an article published in *PLOS One* titled "Plastic Pollution in the World's Oceans: More than 5 Trillion Plastic Pieces Weighing over 250,000 Tons Afloat At Sea," most plastic particles in the ocean are not from large plastics like bags, cups, or straws, but rather from microplastics. Of the 5.25 trillion plastic particles reported to be found in the ocean, about 4.5 trillion are from microplastics.[12] Our clothes contribute to these numbers through two different routes: fibers from these plastic-based fabrics coming off in washing machines and fibers just coming off while we go about our daily routine.

THE MICROPLASTICS IN YOUR DRINKING WATER

An article published in the *Marine Pollution Bulletin* titled "Release of synthetic microplastic plastic fibers from domestic washing machines: effects of fabric type and washing conditions" described the effect that washing clothes has on releasing synthetic fibers. In the study, scientists took three different types of synthetic material: polyester, acrylic, and a polyester-cotton blend, and washed them in a washing machine. They found the acrylic garment to shed the most fibers, totaling at 728,789 fibers per wash. The polyester-cotton

---

11   Brian Resnick, "More than ever, our clothes are made of plastic. Just washing them can pollute the oceans," *Vox*, January 11, 2019.

12   Marcus Erikson et al., "Plastic Pollution in the World's Oceans: More than 5 Trillion Plastic Pieces Weighing over 250,000 Tons Afloat at Sea," *PLoS ONE* 9, no. 12 (2014): e111913.

blend released the least, 137,951 fibers per wash. All these fibers are released as wastewater, which ends up in oceans and other bodies of water.[13]

After the wastewater enters the bodies of water, marine wildlife then ingests the discarded particles. A 2017 study published in *Frontiers* titled "Frequency of Microplastics in Mesopelagic Fishes from the Northwest Atlantic" examined the microplastic content in the gut of fish. Of the 233 fish examined, 73% were found to have microplastics in their stomachs.[14] While we can easily overlook how marine life is affected, the negative impact ultimately comes back to us. Not only are marine ecosystems affected, but we eat these fish, so we also consume these microplastics.

We also ingest microplastics through our drinking water. Another study, published in the *Marine Pollution Bulletin,* surveyed the Hudson River in New York to assess the number of microplastics in the water. The study found, on average, 0.98 microplastics per liter. This pollution affects not only marine life, but also human health.

The Hudson River is not the only site of contamination. In 2019, a study published in *Groundwater* titled "Microplastic Contamination in Karst Groundwater Systems" found micro-plastic contamination in springs and wells from groundwater

---

13   Imogen E. Napper and Richard C. Thompson, "Release of synthetic microplasic fibers from domestic washing machine: Effects of fabric type and washing conditions," *Marine Pollution Bulletin* 112, no. 1-5 (2016): 39-45.

14   Alina M. Wieczorek et al., "Frequency of Microplastics in Mesopelagic Fishes from the Northwest Atlantic," *Frontiers in Marine Science* 5, (2018): 39.

systems in Illinois. The source for the microplastic contamination was fibers with a concentration of 15.2 microplastic particles per liter.[15]

Groundwater systems are a major source of fresh water, which is drinkable water. According to an article published in *PLOS* titled "Anthropogenic contamination of tap water, beer, and sea salt," debris was found in 81 percent of tap water sources. 98.3 percent of the debris particles found in the tap water were fibers.[16] The thought of ingesting clothing fibers is unsettling.

Few studies explore the negative effects of ingesting microplastics, but concern surrounds this conversation. The National Institutes of Health explains that microplastics could adversely affect human health as plastic contains toxic ingredients.[17]

DYEING PLANTS AND TOXIC WATER SOURCES

Not only do the fibers in textiles pollute our water sources, but the dye that gives garments their vibrant color produces detrimental effects as well. A study published in the *Journal of Environmental Management* reports that wastewater released from textile-dyeing plants is highly toxic. Additionally, wastewater contains organic and inorganic compounds,

---

15   Samuel V Panno et al., "Microplastic Contamination in Karst Groundwater Systems," *Groundwater* 57, no. 2 (2019): 189-196.

16   Mary Kosuth, Sherri A. Mason, and Elizabeth V. Wattenberg, "Anthropogenic contamination of tap water, beer and sea salt," *PLoS One* 13, no. 4 (2018): e0194970.

17   "Microplastics," National Institutes of Health, accessed May 4, 2020.

including toxic heavy metals, carcinogenic amines, surfactants, and disinfectants—substances that are all harmful for human consumption.[18]

Citarum River, located in Indonesia, is one water source that is feeling the effects of the pollution of textile dyeing plants. The World Bank considers the Citarum River to be the most polluted river in the world.[19] It is the site where dyeing plants in the city of Majalaya dump their waste. Majalaya is a major location for textile production, and reportedly produces 40 percent of the country's textiles. Citarum River is the place where locals fish, wash their clothes, and tend to other daily needs. As a result, people are experiencing adverse side effects. Channel News Asia reports that the locals using the water experience hair loss and have itchy skin.[20]

In 2018, *Al Jazeera* reported the struggles that civilians experience while using water from the Citarum River for their daily needs. One woman named Nour uses water for everyday tasks such as bathing, washing dishes, and washing vegetables.[21] She describes the water as black or red, and she feels that her children are always sick because of it. Families like Nour's have no choice but to use the Citarum River to fulfill their daily needs. They should not be exposed to

---

18 Katarzyna Paździor et al., "Influence of ozonation and biodegradation on toxicity of industrial textile wastewater," *Journal of Environmental Management* 195, no. 2 (2017): 166-173.

19 Guy Hutton, "Cleaning Up One of the World's Most Polluted Places," *World Bank Blogs,* December 19, 2013.

20 Chandni Vatvani. "The toxic waste that enters Indonesia's Ciatrum River, one of the World's Most Polluted," *Channel News Asia,* April 14, 2018.

21 "Indonesia's Most Polluted river," *Al Jazeera,* May 03, 2018.

dangerous chemicals, especially not when fulfilling such a basic necessity like water use.

While the affected countries seem light-years away from the United States, those chemicals eventually find their way back to us when we wash our clothes. Additionally, we are connected to these countries globally. These polluted water sources overseas eventually find their way into larger bodies of water, like oceans. The Citarum river flows into the Java Sea, a body of water surrounding Indonesia and Malaysia. This is not just one country's issue; this is a global problem.

Fast fashion may provide an avenue for the average fashion-lover to emulate the styles of their favorite influencer, but it comes at a higher cost. Cheap labor and material are detrimental to us as a whole. It's time to look for alternatives to how we make our clothing and the materials that we use for these processes. It's time to be smarter consumers. Our planet and fundamental human rights demand it. If we want to make a difference, we need to start investing in alternatives now. Biofabrication provides the perfect solution.

CHAPTER 2

THE HISTORY OF FASHION IN THE UNITED STATES OF AMERICA

Before exploring what the future of fashion and biology has in store, we must go back to the basics. How were we producing and wearing apparel before fast fashion ideology took over? The practices that preceded today's industry give insight into sustainable ways to create material and allow us to consider ideas that increase the durability and strength of a material, while still maintaining a smooth, fabric feel.

NATIVE AMERICAN IDEOLOGY AND TECHNOLOGY
Native Americans were the first people to live in the Americas. The relationship they have with the land was that they hope to preserve and protect it. The definition of the word 'nature' in the Native American sense is the connection one has with the land and the approach one has when using its natural resources. In contrast, the Eurocentric definition of

the word refers to the physical world that is entirely separate from the individual, and the individual is prioritized above the land.[22] While this definition may seem irrelevant to the topic of fashion, these differing ideologies explain the approach of today's fast fashion industry and how we need to change the current perspective we have of the environment.

This respectful ideology extended to how Native Americans interact with the environment and how they use its resources. For example, historically, when they hunted an animal, they would use the entirety of the remains. They ate the meat, and they used animal skins such as deerskin, buckskin, buffalo, rabbit, and bearskin to create textiles for their clothing. In order to prepare the skins to be worn as clothing, Native Americans would use the process of tanning and smoking the hides. Tanning made the hides soft and pliable, so they became easy to work with and comfortable to wear. This process was necessary because leather that is not tanned will rot, which would be a total fashion faux pas.[23]

From a 21st century perspective, the disadvantage of tanning is that it takes a few days, which is longer than the time it takes for me to get my Amazon prime shipments. Thus, it's not the best way to appease the modern, fashionable consumer.

22   Padraig Kirwan, "The Emergent Land: Nature and Ecology in the Native American Expressive Forms," English Department of California Davis, 1999.

23   "How is Leather Tanned?" Best Leather (blog), accessed December 30, 2019. Best Leather (blog).

THE PROCESS OF CREATING SOFT BUCKSKIN

The Choctaw Native Americans created durable and soft buckskin, called "tvlhko" in Choctaw language, by tanning deer hides. Prior to the tanning process, the hides were stripped of the hair, meat, and flesh. The hide was placed in water and wood ashes for a few days, killing bacteria, and making it easier to soften later in the tanning process. Afterwards, the hide was left for a day in a stream to wash away the wood ashes and bring the hide back to a neutral pH.[24]

The process of turning the hide into leather involved chemicals called emulsified oils, which came from animal brains, corn mush, and egg yolks. Water and emulsified oil were mixed and heated to create a hot water bath. The hides were soaked in this solution. Then, they were wrung out to begin the process of softening them. While the hide was drying, it needed to be stretched to ensure that it would dry soft. The stretching of the hide and the emulsified oils prevented the fibers in the hide from forming natural bonds, which would result in a hard and stiff hide.[24]

There were three different techniques for stretching the hide. The most basic method was turning and pulling it with one's hands and knees. Another method was taking the hide and putting it on a frame, then using a tool to push forcefully into the hide, covering every part of it. The third method involved placing the tool used for softening in the ground and stretching the hide back and forth over it. Regardless of the softening technique of choice, this process took hours and required diligence because if any part of the hide dried

---

24 "Traditional Buckskin," *Biskink,* December 30, 2019.

stiff, then the hide would have to be soaked in emulsified oil and the entire process would have to be repeated.[24]

If a hide became wet after going through this process, it returned back to the stiff state of a rawhide. To prevent it from stiffening when wet, it was put through the process of smoking.[24]

Smoking hides prevented them from returning to a stiff state because the smoke used contained formaldehyde. Another advantage of smoking the hide is that it also protected the resulting buckskin from bugs that would want to eat the material. The source used to smoke the hides determined the resulting color of the buckskin: corncob smoke made it yellow; oak bark made it dark brown; alder bark made it reddish-brown.[24]

The smoked buckskin could also be dyed with plant materials like walnut hulls. Walnut hulls were significant because they are high in tannic acid, which not only dyes the buckskin to a dark color, but it also makes it less stretchy, less water absorbent, and further protects the buckskin from bugs. After this process, the buckskin was ready to be made into a pair of moccasins, a robe, a skirt, bags, and many other items.[24]

COMMON RESOURCES: PLANT FIBERS AND MOSS

A material that was popular to use for garments and textiles amongst Native Americans in the regions between Virginia and southeastern Texas was Spanish moss. Spanish moss trees were found along rivers, so a canoe was used, and the moss was harvested from forked poles. Before use, the moss was smoked with aromatic fires to kill the insects that resided within it. Afterward, the plants were spun by spindles to create mats, blankets, fringe, and skirts for women. Women preferred to wear Spanish moss skirts over deer hide because of the heat and humidity of the south. A *tarabe* tool was used to weave Spanish moss amongst the Houma, Koasati, and Alibamu tribes. This was adopted from the Europeans and used to twist together cords of Spanish moss.[25]

Another technique Native Americans used to weave together different plant fibers like elm trees, milkweed, and Indian hemp was finger weaving. Basswood bark was another source of plant fibers. The bark was cut from the tree using an ax. Then, the bark was loosened with a knife so it could be pulled off in long strips by one's hands. The strips were then rolled up to be transported for further preparation. Afterward, the strips were boiled with hardwood ashes and further separated with a knife. The fibers were then run over stones to soften them. After all this, the fibers were dyed using plants and minerals, resulting in fibers that were yellow, blue, black, or reddish-brown. The way in which the fibers were weaved depended on the end-use of the product. The process of finger weaving began by tying fibers of different lengths to a tree. The fibers were woven together by hand, (as the name of the process implies) taking strands under and over each other.[26]

While Native Americans were able to establish a strong connection with the land through these methods, the time it took

---

25   Max Carocci, "Clad with the 'Hair of Trees': A History of Native American Moss Textile Industries," *Textile History* 41, no. 1 (2013): 3-27.

26   Native American Art: Native American Finger Weaving in the Eastern Forests," Suzanne Dalton (blog), accessed December 20, 2019.

to create textiles and fabrics could not meet the needs of consumers in postcolonial and colonial America. The demand for quicker clothing created a drastic change in its textile industry through the industrial revolution.

THE INDUSTRIAL REVOLUTION

Inventions such as John Kay's flying shuttles, Eli Whitney's cotton gin, and James Hargreaves's spinning jenny revolutionized how the Western world produced clothing—increasing production to unimaginable heights. The spinning jenny allowed one worker to spin 120 spools at a time. This led Great Britain to surpass India as the world's leading cotton producer.[27]

While the Industrial Revolution allowed the Western world to outcompete other countries in production and economics, many disadvantages resulted from it as well. The main sources of fuel for factories were nonrenewable resources such as coal and natural gas. Before, the energy used came naturally from plants and animals and recycled throughout the ecosystem through the food web. The Industrial Revolution broke that recycling through the introduction of this new type of fuel—one that has no way of being reused.[7]

Additionally, the conditions and treatment of factory workers were poor. They worked long hours for low pay in dangerous and dirty working conditions. Dangerous parts of machines were left unguarded, which left workers at risk of serious

---

27 *CrashCourse*, "Coal, Steam, and the Industrial Revolution: Crash Course World History #32," August 30, 2012, video, 11:05.

injuries. Child labor was also a widespread practice. Children younger than the age of 9 could be found working in these conditions.[28]

TODAY'S FASHION INDUSTRY AND ITS FUTURE

While we like to believe the fashion and textile industry has separated itself from these practices, this is far from the truth. Child labor is no longer legal in the United States, but companies outsource to other parts of the world. According to a report published by the International Labour Organization, 170 million children work in textile factories that create garments to appease America and Europe's infatuation with fast fashion.[29] Clearly, not much has changed from 300 years ago.

In addition to these unethical labor practices, the fast fashion industry also uses practices that are detrimental to the environment. For example, creating a jacket requires about 10,330 liters of water.[30] One person can use that amount of water for 24 years. Additionally, companies that create fabrics like viscose obtain their materials from ancient or threatened forests, and only 30 percent of the materials they collect actually goes into making the fabric.[31]

28   "Working Conditions during the Industrial Revolution," History Crunch (blog), last modified July 29 2019.

29   Josephine Moulds, "Child labour in the fashion supply chain," *The Guardian,* n.d.

30   *The Patriot Act,* "The Ugly Truth of Fashion | The Patriot Act," November 25, 2019, video, 29:02.

31   "Rayon (Viscose)," Council of Fashion Designers of America, accessed August 24, 2020.

There are so many detrimental effects that textile production creates in the fast fashion industry—clearly, something needs to change in the way we are producing clothes. Suzanne Lee proposes the next revolution is biofabrication. We should not compromise our health, our ethics, and the environment for fashion. We can do this without giving up our appreciation for fashionable aesthetics. As Lee says, "We need a material revolution, and we need it now."[32]

32 Suzanne Lee, "Why Biofabrication is the Next Industrial Revolution," Filmed July 2019 at TEDSummit, Edinburg, Scotland, video, 12:12.

CHAPTER 3

WHAT IS BIOFABRICATION?

Biofabrication. It sounds like a made-up word. My computer doesn't accept it as a word. Google Docs doesn't accept it as a word. An angry red squiggly line underlines every occurrence of it. No definition for biofabrication lives on the Merriam Webster website or Dictionary.com, so it has to be made up, right? Clearly, this term has not yet been accepted in the English language, but in the scientific world, it encompasses a variety of definitions depending on its application.

CREATING CRYSTALS WITH BIOFABRICATION

The first documented occurrence of biofabrication is in a 1994 journal article about using biomineralization to create pearls. Biomineralization refers to the process of creating small particles like minerals and crystals. This article focuses on biofabricating a flat pearl through a process that is similar to the growth of a natural pearl. They recreate this natural growth by placing glass, mica, and molybdenum disulfide between the shell and mantle of *Haliotis rufescens*, a species of sea snail. They recreated this natural process using an organism as the vehicle of production.[33]

COMBINING BIOLOGY AND ELECTRONICS

In 2010, another article explored the concept of biofabrication through building 'bio-device' interfaces that could transform medicine through identifying pathogens and diagnosing diseases. It presents the challenge that electronic devices are incompatible with natural biological systems, proposing biofabrication as a possible solution in the integration of the two. The article describes using materials that respond to stimuli and utilizing the existing biological framework to assist with development. For example, our DNA contains the blueprint for the millions of cells that make us up. Using this existing biological tool, maybe we can figure out ways to create a compatible biological and electronic environment at the cellular level. The article compares biofabrication to a toolbox that will constantly increase in tools in the future, and emphasizes that we can use those tools to achieve the unimaginable.[34]

BIOFABRICATION IN MEDICINE

In the realm of tissue engineering, biofabrication refers to using cells as the tools to generate three dimensional models

---

33 Monika Fritz et al., "Flat Pears from Biofabrication of Organized Composites on Inorganic Substrates," *Nature* 371, no. 6495 (1994): 49-51.

34 Yi Liu et al., "Biofabrication to build the biology-device interface," *Biofabrication* 2, no. 2 (2010).

of tissue. An interesting characteristic of tissue engineering biofabrication is bioassembly, a process in which cells fibers are weaved together like the way fibers are weaved to make a textile. Tissue engineering biofabrication encompasses bioprinting as well, which explores the three-dimensional and two-dimensional orientation of cells. While bioassembly and bioprinting seem to have similar definitions, we can differentiate between these two terms through their focus. Bioassembly focuses on utilizing cells as materials to create tissue, while bioprinting focuses on the spatial arrangement of the cells. Additionally, bioassembly occurs at the cellular level, while bioprinting occurs at the molecular level. Biofabrication uses existing biological elements to innovate and enhance our body.[35] This type of technology could potentially save the lives of millions of patients waiting for an organ. The patient would not have to wait for an organ donor. Instead, biofabrication could allow scientists to grow the desired organ in a lab from the patient's cells.

Growing organs is not just a possibility for the future. Scientists are experimenting with these possibilities now. In 2019, a report was published on recreating the parts of the human heart by bioprinting collagen. Collagen is a protein that is found throughout our bodies: in skin, muscles, bones, organs, and other connective tissues.[36] In the report, the scientists used a method called FRESH, freeform reversible embedding of suspending hydrogels to bioprint collagen, and were able

---

35 Jürgen Groll et al., "Biofabrication: reappraising the definition the definition of an evolving field," *Biofabrication* 8, no. 1 (2016).

36 "The Best Way You Can Get More Collagen," Cleveland Clinic Health Essentials, "The Best Way You Can Get More Collagen," May 15, 2018, accessed May 11, 2020.

to recreate parts of a heart that were specific to a patient's anatomy.[37] This illustrates the potential of biofabrication, and that potential expands beyond just the medical field.

I know a lot of this seems like something you would read in a science fiction novel. It's pretty cool, right? Although these scientific fields have drastically different applications of biofabrication, they have three basic similarities. Scientist Xiaolong Luo summarizes these three similarities: "First, the building blocks are cells or biologics; second, the fabrication processes are bio-inspired or bio-friendly; and finally, the products are biological systems, models or devices with transformative properties." From this description, biofabrication is creating a product through a biological process. While "bio" is only a small part of the word, the essence of biofabrication is biology.[38]

BIOFABRICATION IN THE FASHION INDUSTRY (FINALLY!)

Okay, so you can make tissues, technology, and minerals with biofabrication, but what does this have to do with fashion? What does biofabrication mean for the fashion world?

We can define it the same way as the other sciences—creating textile or dyes using a biological process. Currently, plenty of

---

37 Andrew Lee et al., "3D Bioprinting of collagen to rebuild components of the human heart," *Science* 365, no. 6452 (2019): 482-487.

38 Luo, Xiaolong, "Biofabrication in Microfluidics: A Converging Fabrication Paradigm to Exploit Biology in Microsystems," *Journal of Bioengineering and Biomedical Science* 2, no. 2 (2012).

companies and projects develop textiles, material, and dyes through biological means.

Suzanne Lee explored the realm of biofabrication when she grew material for her jacket from bacteria. Lee's bacteria jacket led her to seek out other ways biofabrication could be used in the fashion industry. She founded Biofabricate, a community for startups, investors, and brands hoping to create a more sustainable future for fashion with biotechnology.[39]

At a talk with the *Business of Fashion*, Andras Forgacs, the cofounder of Modern Meadow, says "Biofabrication is a discipline that sits at the intersection of biology engineering, and design… which allows us to go back to some of our most ancient materials… and reinterpret them."[40] Forgacs's company grows leather using bacteria, reimagining the traditional route of creating leather with animal hides.

The implications of biofabrication go beyond just creating sustainable materials. They also reimagine how we interact with our clothes. In 2017, researchers at MIT created a workout suit with microbes. The suit consists of flaps lined with microbes. The microbes respond to changes in humidity by shrinking or expanding. When the person wearing the suit starts sweating, the flaps will open.[41] This creates a symbiotic relationship between the clothes and the wearer.

---

39 "Biofabricate is a platform for biomaterial innovators and consumer brands growing a sustainable," Biofabricate, accessed May 11, 2020.

40 *The Business of Fashion,* "Welcome to the Era of Biofabrication | Andras Forgacs | #BoFVOICES 2017," April 23, 2018, video, 23:51.

41 Jennifer Chu, "Researchers Design Moisture-Responsive Workout Suit," *MIT News,* May 19, 2017.

Biofabrication will allow the fashion industry to rethink not only how to design clothing, but also our relationship with the clothes that we wear.

Biofabrication is the future of the fashion industry. Biofabrication provides a better, more environmentally friendly manufacturing process to the current production habits of the fashion industry. By using biological materials, manufacturers use tools that are naturally occurring and already biodegradable. This provides a solution to the current waste production that results from manufacturing clothes and accessories in fashion. If we want to create a more sustainable future, we need to start rethinking the way we make our materials. Biofabrication provides that alternative and it will revolutionize the way we make and wear clothing.

PART 2

THE BIOFABRICATION AGE

In 2018 at Voices, a conference held by the *Business of Fashion,* CEO of Modern Meadow, Andras Forgacs established that human civilization evolves through the way in which they create and obtain materials. British Material Scientist Mark Midownik perfectly captures the idea of this evolution. He says, "The story of materials is the story of civilization."[42]

In the preceding chapter, we discussed the history of fashion and how materials were created throughout civilizations in America and the world. The Native Americans collected their materials directly from nature. Then, in the Industrial Revolution, the production of materials was upscaled. Now, we need a new kind of revolution; one that allows us to both produce and manufacture materials at a larger scale, and one that is sustainable.

Biofabrication is the next phase, and this era has just begun. This phase of the revolution is precisely why it's important to examine companies such as Modern Meadow, Bolt Threads and more. How are they bioengineering fabrics? Where will this take the fashion industry?

42   *The Business of Fashion,* "Welcome to the Era of Biofabrication | Andras Forgacs | #BoF Voices 2017," April 23, 2018, video, 23:51.

CHAPTER 4

GROWING LEATHER WITH MODERN MEADOW

Leather is a staple in every fashionista's wardrobe. Whether it's a leather bag, leather jacket, leather boot, or a pair of leather pants (if you really want to make a statement), leather is one textile that can up your fashion game, but at what cost? In 2016, an article published in *The Guardian* reported that 290 million cows are slaughtered annually to fulfill the demands of the leather industry.[43] There must be another way to satisfy the demand for this textile. Modern Meadow presents an alternative to this mindless slaughter of cattle— growing leather with the help of biology's most basic unit: the cell.

Before CEO Andras Forgacs co-founded Modern Meadow, he and his father founded Organova, a biotech company that 3D prints human organs and tissues. According to the *Business*

---

43   Lucy Siegle, "Is it Time to Give Up Leather?" *The Guardian,* March 13, 2016.

of Fashion, Organova creates skin models that are used for cosmetic testing at beauty brands like L'Oréal.[44] Already experienced with biofabricating organs and tissues in the medical realm, Forgacs took his knowledge from printing organs and applied it to creating one of fashion's most coveted and controversial items.

THE ENVIRONMENTAL IMPACT

The Guardian projected that the leather industry would have to slaughter 430 million cows annually by the year 2025 if it wanted to meet the production demands of creating luxury wallets, handbags, shoes, etc.[43] Our love for leather should not lead to the extinction of cows. The leather industry's current practices are excessive and focused on meeting consumer demands while ignoring the greater implications.

Another major environmental impact of the leather industry is the greenhouse gases that it produces. According to an article published in *Energy Procedia* titled "Analyzing the Carbon Footprint of the Finished Bovine Leather: A Case Study of Aniline Leather," in Taiwan, the total carbon emissions for obtaining raw hides is 73 kg of CO_2 per cubic meter. Annually, that is 26,645 kg of CO_2 per cubic meter.[45]

Let's compare the carbon footprint of the Taiwanese leather industry to the carbon footprint of an average person in Taiwan for reference. *Taipei Times* reports that, in 2011, the

---

44 "Andras Forgacs," Business of Fashion, accessed May 9, 2020.

45 Kuo-Wen Chen, Lung-Chieh Lin, and Wen-Shing Lee, "Analyzing the Carbon Footprint of Finished Bovine Leather," *Energy Procedia* 61, (2014): 1063-1066.

average person in Taiwan had a daily carbon footprint of 19.6 kg. This is four times more than the number recommended by the UN.[46,47] To compare, a day of obtaining raw hides is about three times what the average person uses in Taiwan.

The average person in Taiwan already exceeds the recommended daily carbon footprint by a factor of four, which means that the Taiwanese leather industry's carbon footprint is seven times greater than the UN's recommended value. These figures cannot be dismissed. These values add up and, ultimately, they contribute to environmental issues like global warming. While the Taiwanese leather industry is on the other side of the world, these figures can give us a better idea of the environmental cost, worldwide.

The greenhouse gas emissions that come from simply producing and obtaining raw hides already greatly exceeds the UN's recommended daily carbon footprint value, but these figures do not take raising the livestock into account. According to the Food and Agriculture Organization, the total CO_2 emissions from livestock globally is 7.1 million tons.[47] Compared to production of leather, raising livestock is a much greater contributor to greenhouse gas emissions. The leather industry cannot continue these negative environmental impacts.

The alternative that Modern Meadow presents eliminates the steps of raising cattle, slaughtering cows, and obtaining

---

46 "Taiwan outproduces East Asia in Carbon Emissions," *Taipei Times,* October 14, 2011.

47 "Key Facts and Findings" Food and Agriculture Organization of the United Nations, accessed May 9, 2020.

rawhides altogether. Forgacs describes the process that Modern Meadow employs to create leather in his 2013 Ted Talk titled "Leather and meat without killing animals." Forgacs explains, "…animal products are just collects of tissues, and right now we breed and raise highly complex animals only to create products that are made of relatively simple tissues. What if, instead of starting with a complex, sentient animal, we started out with what tissues are made of, the basic unit of life, the cell?"[48]

MODERN MEADOW'S BIOLOGICAL SOLUTION

Forgacs presents this idea in his Ted Talk, describing a process of obtaining leather where no animals are killed. The process of growing the leather begins by taking cells from animals. This could be any animal; it does not have to be a cow. Through this simple process, no animals are harmed. The cells that are extracted from the animal are isolated, and then placed in a cultured medium where they multiply, producing billions of other cells. After the cells have multiplied, the cells in the culture are put in conditions that are favorable for producing collagen.[48]

THE PROTEIN

Collagen is a protein, and according to the National Institutes of Health, it is the most abundant protein in animals. The function of collagen is to provide structural support as

---

48   Andras Forgacs, "Leather and Meat without killing animals," Filmed June 2013 at TedGlobal 2013, Edinburg, Scotland, video, 8:35.

it makes up connective tissue and the extracellular matrix.[49] The extracellular matrix is a term that refers to the proteins and molecules that hold the cells together.[49] Collagen is important for creating leather because this tissue makes up the 'traditional' leather that is used to create our bags, shoes, and wallets.

After the cells have produced the collagen, both the cells and collagen are spread out to form sheets. These sheets are layered on top of each other to form thicker sheets and left to mature. Once the thick sheet has matured, it is taken through a shorter, less chemical tanning process, which creates the leather. The great part about this process is that it gives designers full control of what they want the end product to look like. For example, in this process, a transparent leather can be created with seven sheets of cells and collagen. An opaque leather can be created with twenty-one sheets of collagen.[50]

YEAST CELLS: THE NEW BIOLOGICAL FACTORIES

When Modern Meadow was founded in 2012, its goal was to bioengineer both materials and meat. In 2013, Modern Meadow shifted its focus to creating materials. Currently, Modern Meadow employs a similar process, but they do not use animal cells—they use yeast cells. These yeast cells are obtained from cell banks that provide cells to other industries like beer breweries and pharmaceutical companies.

---

49 Matthew D. Shoulders and Ronald T. Raines, "Collagen Structure and Stability," *Annual Review of Biochemistry*, 78 (2009): 929-958.

50 Andras Forgacs, "Leather and Meat without killing animals," Filmed June 2013 at TedGlobal 2013, Edinburg, Scotland, video, 8:35.

They take the DNA of these ordinary yeast cells and manipulate it so that they have the ability to produce collagen. They produce collagen through fermentation, which is a common method for brewing beer, making insulin, and making bread.[50] After the collagen has been produced, it is sent to be purified and made into sheets where it can be prepared and manufactured into many different types of products. The process of growing this leather takes two weeks.[51]

Compare this to the way we create leather traditionally—if we account for all the time it takes to raise livestock and process the hides, it takes years. At Modern Meadow, the feed stock for the yeast comes from glycerol, which is one of the products in biodiesel production. The company hopes to use materials and resources that are environmentally friendly. On their website, they emphasize this commitment. "Our technology can support other bio-source feedstocks as well. As we scale, we can target the best feedstock for a specific production region that reduces land use, fresh-water use and [greenhouse gas] emissions."[52] At all levels, biofabricating leather from yeast cells is more efficient, sustainable, and fashionable (because being sustainable is always in fashion).

ZOA: A NEW LIFE FOR LEATHER

Modern Meadow hopes to debut their commercial product, which is called Zoa™ within the next year. Zoa™ was initially launched on September 26, 2017, and a prototype shirt was created for the MOMA exhibit "Items: Is Fashion Modern?"

---

51 "FAQ," Modern Meadow, accessed May 9, 2020.
52 Ibid.

The t-shirt was black with large white shapes. The pattern is reminiscent of one you would imagine on a cow. The name for Zoa™ is derived from Zoey, or the Greek word for life. The Modern Meadow website describes the Zoa™ product as "inspired by leather."[53]

Forgacs points out that this gives designers more creative liberty. In a Ted Talk, he says, "And because we make this material from the ground up, we can control its properties in very interesting ways."[54] Biofabrication gives more freedom in not just the look of the leather, but also its other characteristics as well, like durability and softness. The biofabrication of leather eliminates the need to skin the hides and take out the hairs from it. Additionally, the hides that are skinned come in the shape of the cow, and the raw hides can have holes and scars from insect bites. With biofabrication, the leather does not have these imperfections.

Animal leather does not give designers the ability to dictate the feel and style like yeast leather allows. Biofabricating leather allows designers to focus on making their vision come alive, rather than the environmental impacts and the limitations that come with working with a hide skinned from an animal. In his Ted Talk, Forgacs says, "We can mimic nature, but in some ways improve upon it. This type of leather can do what today's leather does, but with imagination, probably much more."[6] With more control over the feel and the look

---

53   Gayathri Kesar, "Material Story: Zoa," *Material Connexion,* January 9, 2018.

54   Andras Forgacs, "Leather and Meat without killing animals," Filmed June 2013 at TedGlobal 2013, Edinburg, Scotland, video, 8:35.

of the leather, the leather that is made can be catered to what the final product will be, whether that is a jacket or shoes.

Growing leather with yeast cells will completely transform the leather industry. We won't have to sacrifice cows for the sake of fashion. Additionally, it will completely eliminate the greenhouse gas emissions that go into creating leather. Biotechnology transformed something as small as a cell into a factory for producing raw materials for making leather.

We can wear our favorite leather pieces guilt-free.

CHAPTER 5

REFASHIONING FIBERS WITH BOLT THREADS

Polyester, nylon, and acrylic are some synthetic fibers with which we are familiar. All these fibers are plastic based and contribute to the microplastic pollution that ends up in our drinking water (yuck!).[55] We need to rethink what goes into these synthetic fibers and develop better alternatives. We don't have to completely shift to natural fibers, but rather use biofabrication to recreate some of nature's strongest fibers.

Bolt Threads sought to create one alternative by studying one of nature's strongest fibers: spider silk. According to an article published in *Prion* titled "The Elaborate Structure of Spider Silk," when comparing major ampullate silk (MA silk), which refers to the silk made from spiders in the major ampullate gland, to other strong material, they found that

---

55   Kristen Gilbride, "You're Wearing Plastic: The Synthetic Plastic Takeover," Global Fashion Exchange (blog), April 16, 2019.

the synthetic fibers were stronger, while the natural fibers like MA silk were more elastic.[56]

The strength of a substance refers to its ability to endure a force like tension. Looking at the different strengths, MA silk has a strength of 1.1 gigapascals, while steel has a strength of 1.5 gigapascals.[56] While steel has a greater strength, MA silk's strength is not too far behind.

Two other measures of substance performance are toughness and elasticity. Toughness refers to how much stress a substance can endure before breaking. Elasticity is a substance's ability to return to its original state after being stretched. When it comes to how elastic and tough steel and MA silk are, MA silk far outperforms steel in both departments. MA silk's elasticity is at 27 percent, while steel's elasticity is 0.8 percent. MA silk's toughness is 180 megajoules per meters cubed, while steel's is just 6 megajoules per meters cubed.[56] With that level of strength, elasticity, and toughness, MA silk is a great contender for creating textiles.

SPIDER SILK THROUGHOUT THE AGES

The fascination with spider silk is not something new. According to an article published in *JSTOR* titled "The Tangled History of Weaving with Spider Silk," in the 1700s, François Xavier Bon de Saint Hilaire bought spider egg sacs from his neighbors (kind of gross, but it's for fashion), and created a

---

56 Lin Romer and Thomas Scheiber, "The elaborate structure of spider silk: structure and function of a natural high performance fiber," *Prion* 2, no. 4 (2008): 154-161.

pair of gloves and stockings from the spider silk.[57] Bon de Saint Hilaire had not entirely perfected his craft, though, as when his designs were given to king Louis XIV, there was a horrible wardrobe malfunction. The spider silk gloves and stockings tore apart.

One hundred years later, a French Jesuit priest, Paul Camboué created a device that allowed him to reel spider silk out of the golden orb weaver's abdomen.[57] His device was called "the guillotine" because of its resemblance to the medieval execution apparatus.[57] The device was wooden, and the spider was put through the hole, where its head and legs were separated from its abdomen.[58] Then, the spider silk was dragged out by touching the spinneret, the gland that produces the silk. Eventually, this led to the creation of the spider silk farm, and in the 1900s a bed canopy woven from the golden orb spiders' threads were showcased at the Paris Exposition.[57] Unfortunately, this was unsuccessful as well. Spiders cannot be farmed because they are cannibalistic. They covered their cages in webs to prevent any other insect from entering their cages and ate each other.

Fast forward to the 21st century, and this fascination has continued, including in the minds of the founders of Bolt Threads. According to a *Forbes* article, in 2004, Dan Widmaier, Cofounder and CEO of Bolt Threads, started studying spider silk in Chris Voigt's lab as a PhD student at the University of California San Francisco.[58] While working in the lab, he met his cofounder David Breslauer. Widmaier and

---

57 Amelia Soth, "The Tangled History of Weaving with Spider Silk," *JSTOR Daily,* November 15, 2018.

Breslauer later met their other cofounder, Ethan Mirsky, who was a graduate student at UCSF at the time. Mirsky was studying the microfluidics of spider silk and contacted Voigt's lab. A few years later, in 2009, the three of them founded a company with the name Refactored Materials.

CREATING SPIDER SILK TODAY

They began by studying spiders: their genome and the properties of the different silks produced. Widmaier told *Forbes* that initially, they tried to harvest the silk from the golden orb weaver spiders just like Paul Camboué in 1800s France. They had the spiders spin webs on hula hoops. That did not work out. "You can't farm spiders, they just eat each other… they didn't make much silk; we couldn't harvest it, so we looked to the modern tools of biotechnology where we use the genetics of the spider to then make that same material, but no spiders."[58]

After researching biofabrication methods, they started studying the different types of spider silk—seven in total. One silk they studied was dragline silk. According to an article in *Scientific America,* dragline silk is seven times stronger than steel at the same diameter.[59] According to an article published in *PNAS*, this silk is composed of two different types of proteins: Spidroin I and II.[60]

---

58   Amy Feldman, "Clothes From A Petri Dish: $700 Million Bolt Threads May Have Cracked the Code On Spider Silk," *Forbes*, August 15, 2018.

59   William K. Purves, "Why is Spider Silk so Strong?," *Scientific America,* October 16, 2006.

60   J. D. van Beek et al., "The molecular structure of spider dragline silk: Folding and orientation of the protein backbone," *Proceedings of the National Academy of Sciences of the United States of America* 99, no. 16 (2002): 10266-10271.

In the 18th, 19th, and 20th centuries, people did not have the knowledge that we do now in biotechnology. Biotechnology is what allowed Bolt Threads to be successful in their endeavor to obtaining spider silk. The process they use to create spider silk is similar to how Modern Meadow creates collagen. It requires taking the DNA of spiders, specifically the part that creates the protein for creating spider silk and putting it into yeast cells. Then, the yeast cells are fermented so they multiply and produce the spider silk protein. Lastly, the protein is purified to make yarn and textiles.[61] Both Modern Meadow and Bolt Threads use yeast cells as the manufacturing unit to produce protein.

While both Bolt Threads and Modern Meadow employ the same process, they are able to complete two distinct products just by changing the protein the yeast produces. These little yeast cells have become factories for production without creating detrimental environmental effects. This shows the potential of manufacturing with biotechnology and presents a new way of creating textiles. With more experimentation, these little factories will transform traditional methods of textile production.

SOME SPIDER SILK PRODUCTS

Bolt Threads' spider silk is called Microsilk™, and it has already made its way into the fashion world. In March 2017, they launched a tie, which instantly sold out. The necktie was priced at $314.[61] They also teamed up with Best Made

---

61   "Bolt Technology- Meet Microsilk™," Bolt Threads, accessed May 24, 2020.

Co to create knit hats which were priced at $198.[61] In October 2017, Bolt Threads collaborated with Designer Stella McCartney and debuted a golden Microsilk™ dress at MOMA in New York.[61] In 2019, they teamed up with Stella McCartney and Adidas to create a biodegradable tennis dress made from Microsilk™ and a cellulose blend fiber.[61]

CHALLENGES

While Bolt Threads has gotten to collaborate with big designers like Stella McCartney and launch their own products in the past few years, they did not achieve this success overnight. *Forbes* reports that they first received funding in 2011, when Steve Vassallo from Foundation Capital contacted them via LinkedIn.[4] To attract more investors, Breslauer also contacted Lillian Whipple, a local weaver. She wove a swatch with the spider silk.[62]

Bolt Threads overcame setbacks with working with spider silk. In the beginning, they received feedback that their textiles looked "like a sick animal," and another textile melted away in a few days.[4] Another issue they initially ran into was that the material would shrink by 40 percent when put into water. This is due to super contraction, which is a property of spider webs. Jamie Bainbridge, the Vice President of Product Development at Bolt Threads, created a wool and cellulose fiber blend that allowed the textile to retain the properties of the spider silk.[62]

---

62   Amy Feldman, "Clothes From A Petri Dish: $700 Million Bolt Threads May Have Cracked the Code On Spider Silk," *Forbes,* August 15, 2018.

Although these properties of the initial batch of spider silk textiles seem unfavorable, they can be applied to other types of garments in which a shrinking asset would be favorable.

GROWING LEATHER WITH MUSHROOMS

Bolt Threads was able to solve the centuries-long question of how to commercialize spider silk, and now they use their successes to explore other types of biomaterials. They have created another textile, Mylo™.[63] Mycelium cells make up mushrooms. The Bolt Threads website describes the process in which mycelium cells are grown on organic matter. These cells form a three-dimensional network. Finally, this three-dimensional network is tanned and dyed to be made into the final product: Mylo™.[63]

Like Microsilk™, Bolt Threads has had a few collaborations using Mylo™ as well. In April 2018, Bolt Threads collaborated with Stella McCartney to a create a Mylo™ prototype of her Falabella bag, which was showcased at an exhibit in the Victoria and Albert Museum in London.[63] They also partnered with designer Chester Wallace to create the Mylo™ Driver Bag.[63] This was the first commercial Mylo™ product, and the Kickstarter campaign raised $72,285 for the launch of the bag.[64]

The Mylo™ textile looks just like leather and is better than traditional synthetic leathers, which are made from polyurethane—a plastic-based material.[8] It takes less time to grow

---

63   "Bolt Technology-Meet Mylo™," Bolt Threads, accessed May 24, 2020.

64   "This 'leather' bag is animal-free and not petroleum based!," Kickstarter, accessed May 24, 2020.

Mylo™ compared to traditional animal hides. Mylo™ grows in only weeks.[63]

Textiles like Mylo™ and Microsilk™ demonstrate biotechnology's potential to develop textiles for high end fashion—textiles that are just as stylish, and in demand by consumers. Almost every product Bolt Threads has launched has been a hit; it all sells out. Designers and consumers do care about the material that goes into clothing, and the more bio-tech companies are able to receive the proper funding for developing textiles research, the more these technologies can be brought into the mainstream and become common industrial practice.

CHAPTER 6

MYCOWORKS - MAKING LEATHER FROM MUSHROOMS

When looking for fashion's next textiles, we need not look further than what already surrounds us—nature. Think about it for a second. Take a nice walk in the park, and what do you see? A whole group of mushrooms growing at the base of a tree. Maybe your first thought won't be "These mushrooms would make a great textile" but I think it should be.

According to an article published in the Common Objective, the leather industry measures high on the Higg Materials Sustainability Index, which means it has major environmental impacts, including contributing to global warming and high water use.[65] In addition, forests are cleared and land becomes overused simply to raise livestock. According to

---

65 "Fibre Briefing: Leather," Common Objective, February 1, 2018, accessed September 13, 2020.

PETA, every year, more than 1 billion animals are killed for the leather industry globally.[66] We should not let our love for leather continue like this.

With the fashion industry's insatiable desire for leather, mushroom leather is the perfect alternative. MycoWorks, like Bolt Threads, is exploring the potential of mushrooms to create leather.

FROM MUSHROOMS TO LEATHER

MycoWorks launched their own leather-like mycelium textile called Reishi™. Reishi™, was officially launched at New York Fashion Week in February 2020.[67] Béatrice Amblard is a leather artisan that has worked with a variety of leather skins including ostrich, alligator, and stingray.[67] When working with Reishi™ using traditional techniques, she found the mycelium leather to have all the qualities of the typical leather with which she works.[67] When Amblard was testing the fabric for MycoWorks, she told the company, "Stitching is the true test and we had no problems—it was very, very similar to stitching leather."[67] Reishi™ passed all the leather tests, is made from a more sustainable material, and takes less time to create than traditional animal hide leather. Plus, the making of Reishi™ does not require killing animals. Reishi™ proves itself as a potential textile for the fashion world and, at this rate, it will replace traditional animal leather in the fashion world.

---

66   "Leather: Animals Abused and Killed for their Skins," PETA, accessed September 13, 2020.

67   "Fabricating with Reishi™: Through the eyes of master rather artisan, Béatrice Amblard," Reishi™, accessed May 14, 2020.

Co-founder Phil Ross started working with mushrooms in 1996. In an interview with Andrea Grover, Ross explained how learning about mushrooms helped him connect with nature. "I grew up in New York City, and like a lot of urban people, I felt highly alienated from nature. I wanted to connect, but I really didn't know how… Food and mushrooms were the materials in my proximity, so they were the entry point."[4] Ross worked in restaurants in ranging roles, from a dishwasher to a chef. He also worked in hospice care during the AIDs crisis, where he discovered that the Reishi mushroom is beneficial for the immune system.

Initially, Ross started growing Reishi mushrooms to figure out how to grow them as medicine. While he was learning how to grow them, he wanted to use them as casting material. He explained, "In casting, the amount of time you can work with the material before it sets is called 'open time.' In plaster, that may be five minutes, and in cement that might be a couple of hours. But with mushrooms, the open time is almost as long as you can keep them alive."[68]

As Ross explains, open time is the time in which one can manipulate a material. Comparing the open times of plaster, cement, and mushrooms, mushrooms have the longest time. Thus, you have more time to work with the material and perfect your design. Not only are mushrooms a more sustainable material, they also have more favorable characteristics compared to other traditional material.

---

68   Andrea Grover, "The Future is Fungal: Interview with Phil Ross," *Glasstire*, September 8, 2012.

In his research, Ross found that mushrooms had many interesting characteristics. Growing mushrooms is all about controlling their environment.[68] Mushrooms eat everything. What they cannot eat, they hold. All the cells on a mushroom, except the ones that produce spores, are stem cells—cells that have not undergone cell differentiation.

Cell differentiation is when cells designate into a certain type of cell and perform the functions geared toward that cell type. Since most of a mushroom's cells are stem cells, they can be regrown with a tissue no larger than a fingernail.[69] This quality makes mushrooms the perfect candidate for material. Multiple prototypes for designs can be created by using such a small quantity. One mushroom fingernail piece could grow a dress, another a hat, and another a pair of shoes. Before you know it, you've just created an outfit. The possibilities are endless.

GROWING MUSHROOMS

In a lecture at The New School for Design, Ross described the process of growing mushrooms and their habits. Going back to Louis Pasteur's idea of isolating a pure culture, growing mushrooms requires a completely clean area, devoid of anything living.[70] He recreated this dead space with a Laminar Flow Hood, which filters the air so no microorganisms are hanging around.[70] The process begins by taking a piece of mushroom tissue and placing it in a test-tube with seaweed gelatin; this is called a slant.[70] Ross compares growing fungi

69 *The New School,* "Mycotecture: architecture grown out of mushrooms | Parsons The New School for Design," April 11, 2014, video, 1:15:42.

70 Ibid.

to growing a seedling for a plant. Just like a seedling needs to be taken through more dynamic environments, the small fungal tissue must also be exposed to such environments.[70]

To increase the volume of the small fungal tissue, it is fed more food. To do this, the tissue is cut out of the slant and put it into a more food-like pasteurized rye grain.[70] A week after being but into a jar of rye grain, Ross observed that the fungus consumed all the grain in the space.[70] He explains that the mushroom figures out how long it takes them to digest the food with which they are presented.[5] This can take weeks or even years. Mushrooms are living organisms, so they have minds of their own.

Observing the patterns of their behavior, we can manipulate their environments to guide their growth into the desired shape. The larger you want your mushroom sculpture to be, the more food you present into its environment. "It likes to eat. It likes to grow. It is very much dependent on how you feed it, and learning how to feed it well."[70] Once the mushroom has grown, it releases billions of spores: some land on a tree and immediately start growing, others travel across the globe, and some take a trip into space before finding their spot on the ground.[70]

Another interesting quality of mushrooms is that, when they grow in proximity to one another, they create mechanical "clamp" connections.[70] These connections cause the cell walls of the neighboring mushrooms to fuse together and can occur at any time during the mushroom's life cycle. Ross calls this phenomenon "kind recognition"—the mushrooms recognize their own kind.[70] Ross explains that this is what makes material made from mushrooms so strong. "When a force or some type of energy moves through a mycelium block, it's branching out... It's not going through a solid crystalline structure, but it's going between these types of interconnections."[70] This establishes a strong foundation, which is ideal for any constructive material. Additionally, these connections have the potential to be used as a form of communication. Like the network of neurons in our brains send signals through their synapses, the energy or force that moves through the mycelium blocks could serve the role of signals.

MUSHROOM SCULPTURES

From his research and observations of mushrooms in nature, Ross grew his own structure by joining together the fruits of the mushrooms, deforming them by growing it around objects that the mushrooms would not eat.[70] The fruit of the mushroom is the part that grows out of the ground, while the mycelium is the network of cells underneath.[71] The mycelium cells were put into a box of sawdust, and the fruits would grow out of the box.[71] Growing this structure took three to five years. "It was a very good lesson in aesthetics because I made this remarkable object that took me like five years to grow, but I'd show it to people, and it looked like a used dog's chew toy."[71] While Ross's first sculpture may not have been aesthetically appealing to the public, this sculpture shows our ability to influence the growth patterns of mushrooms and how they are a material with which we can work.

---

71   Ibid.

In 2009, Ross created a sculpture for the Konsulat Dusseldorf Eat Art exhibit in Germany with mycelium bricks.[71] Using basic masonry skills to place the bricks around a bamboo wood framework, the bricks were shaped into an arch.[71] With six hundred mycelium bricks, he created a tea house.[71] Part of the exhibit included taking the bricks apart, and mixing the mushrooms into an herbal tea.[71] While working with these bricks, Ross discovered their resilience and strength. When he used power tools to work on the sculpture, the power tools burned out.[71] This happened because of the immense force that the power tools applied to the bricks.[71] That force then reverberated throughout the mycelium network, and then bounced back to the power tools.[71] Typically when we think of fungi, we think of the soft fruit of the mushrooms that grow from the ground, but the true strength lies underneath, within the networks of the mycelium. Harnessing the strength of these networks creates possibilities for so many different materials and technologies.

If their ability to destroy power tools is not impressive, mushrooms have another interesting ability: they can sharpen knifes. According to the Dorset Wildlife Trust, one species of mushroom, *Piptoporus betulinus* or the Birch polypore, is known as the 'Razorsharp' fungus because its leathery cap was once used to sharpen tools.[72]

MUSHROOM FURNITURE

Ross continued with his artistic endeavors, creating furniture. In 2012, at Workshop Residence in San Francisco, he

---

72 "Birch Polypore," Dorset Wildlife Trust, accessed May 14, 2020.

created two hundred different types of stools using agricultural waste and salvaged wood.[73] "We grew 100% organic California furniture, locally grown in San Fransisco."[73] The fungal part of the stool was primed with shellac.[73] Ross chose shellac as a primer because it is a biodegradable substance.[73] Do not worry, the fungal furniture was not alive. The fungal part of the furniture was baked. His line of furniture was called the Yamanaka series after Japanese Scientist Shigeru Yamanaka, who first displayed his art of the way mushrooms join different materials. In the early 1980s, Yamanaka sought out a patent for using his discoveries for using mycelium to bind together paper.[73] Ross calls his art Mycotecture; "myco" is a Greek prefix meaning relating to fungus.[73]

MUSHROOMS: THE MATERIAL OF THE FUTURE

With all these amazing qualities, mushrooms seem to be the perfect material for almost anything. Ross took his years of research and cofounded MycoWorks in 2013. He was joined by CEO Sophia Wang, who interned for Ross in 2007 while she was getting her PhD at UC Berkeley. The goal of MycoWorks is to create a wide range of materials from mushrooms.

At the Journey Talk Series at Indie Bio, Wang talked about her journey to becoming the CEO of MycoWorks and about the company's framework. "We are taking an abundance of resources, the world's carbon-based waste, agricultural, lumber-based waste, biofuels waste, and converting it with

---

73   *The New School,* "Mycotecture: architecture grown out of mushrooms | Parsons The New School for Design," April 11, 2014, video, 1:15:42.

mushroom mycelium to create an organic biomaterials platform. We are making materials for the world from everything that grows under the sun."[74]

Through using different waste to create the mycelium products, MycoWorks is creating a business model that supports a circular economy. A circular economy is one that tries to detract from the typical ideology of an economy that leads to generating waste to an economy that tries to eliminate it by using waste as a fuel. This is the sustainable alternative to fast fashion's current model, and it will replace it.

Ross emphasizes the potential of fungi material for the future. "This is going to be a gigantic industry. These are not specious claims. This stuff uses much less energy than conventional manufacturing. It eats garbage, or what we call garbage, biowaste."[75] Fungi are nature's natural recyclers. They decompose organic materials in nature. Our definition of waste is their fuel. If we can harness this ability for generating material, we should. This is the better alternative, and our planet will be better for it.

MycoWorks shows us that the best tools for creating material are found in nature. "We are coming to the realization that we have all the resources we need in this world; we just have to discover new ways of using them," Wang says.[74] Everything we need to create material is already out there. We do not need to turn to synthetic plastic alternatives. Researching and using biotechnology will not only allow us to replicate

---

74   *Woven Multimedia,* "Sophia Wang of Mycoworks-Youtube," September 9, 2016, video, 18:27.

75   *SciFri,* "The Fungi in Your Future," November 16, 2016, video, 5:22.

the materials we have grown to love; it will also allow us to enhance them.

Next time you find yourself walking through the woods and come across some mushrooms, think outside the box. Who knows, maybe you've just found the perfect material for your next design.

CHAPTER 7

BIOGARMENTRY- THE LIVING GARMENT

The fashion industry is one of the most polluting industries in the world. According to the World Bank, it is responsible for 10 percent of annual carbon emissions, producing more greenhouse gases than international flying and maritime shipping combined.[76]

What if, rather than just providing an alternative to production, the product became the solution instead? Biogarmentry presents a solution to the CO_2 emissions that result from living our daily lives. Biogarmentry is a garment made from algae and a blend of synthetic biofibers.

---

76 "How Much Do Our Wardrobes Cost the Environment?," The World Bank, accessed September 3, 2020.

THE BREATHING GARMENT

The coolest part about all this is that the garment is alive, so it needs to photosynthesize while you are wearing it. "Basically, you're going to become like portable trees out there, capturing CO_2 and emitting CO_2 so it's like a living breathing textile, but reversing our breathing system," says Roya Aghighi, the designer behind this project. Aghighi, in collaboration with University of British Columbia, created the first prototype for Biogarmentry. Biogarmentry is a textile that not only produces a sustainable alternative but creates a way to manage the greenhouse gas emissions that have been byproducts of our 21st century lives.

With Biogarmentry, Aghighi hopes to produce a garment that changes the way we interact with our clothing. "I realized that the fast fashion, they [have] become something so disposable that…they don't appreciate the textile anymore. It's just like a thing that you just buy as cheap [as possible] and is crazy accessible to everyone." In fast fashion, our relationship with our garments is very short-lived. We see our favorite influencer wear it on Instagram; we buy it and wear it maybe once, and the garment most likely ends up in the landfill a few months later. Biogarmentry challenges this notion. Since this garment is alive, it requires the proper. The garment needs to be sprayed with water to keep the algae alive.

As a designer, Aghighi did not want to contribute to the waste production of the fashion industry. "I'm obsessed with fashion. I love fashion but then, at the same time, I couldn't get my head around how much waste and how much harm we are creating with the fashion and textile industry right now." She did not want to be a designer that contributed to the current ongoing cycle of design, wear, and dispose. "I didn't want to be another fashion designer. I didn't want to contribute to the whole… basically, mess that other designers are creating."

She hoped to tackle two problems: first, to halt the detrimental relationship that fast fashion has created between designer/consumer and clothing; and second, provide a solution to the tangible air pollution. "I am originally from Iran… you could feel the air pollution in your lawn." As a designer, her mind went to fashion—to create a garment that provided both of these solutions.

OUR INTERACTION WITH CLOTHING

Aghighi's idea to make a living garment came from her research on human psychology. Initially, she did a project on depression. Aghighi found the biggest drive for our decisions is guilt, and this emotion is evoked towards our care for living things. "With living things around [you] like your kids, pets, plants, no matter how deep that connection [is], no matter how good a parent you are… you don't want [them] to die; you don't want to kill anything because that guilt is gonna stay with [you] forever." As humans, we do not consciously want to do harm to the living things under our care.

With Biogarmentry, this garment will become another living thing to treat with care. Biogarmentry is interactive. You provide care to it to keep the garment alive, and see that care manifest before you. The algae in the fabric grows as you spray them with water. "All those beautiful green patches start to grow, eventually your whole garment is going to become green. At the end of the cycle, it loses color." There is no such thing as too much water. The research that Aghighi and her team did shows that the algae in the garment like water, so it can be worn out in the rain. Aghighi is also looking into how sweat influences the algae. Some studies show that algae get nutrients from human sweat. With more research, this could potentially be another way to care for the garment.

Before the COVID-19 pandemic, Aghighi was researching how different types of algae would fare growing fibers in the Netherlands at Delft University of Technology with a materials engineering lab supervised by Elvin Karana. Currently, the algae are grown within the fibers on a petri dish. The next step of the project is to get it beyond the petri dish, surviving beyond the lab once it's with the consumer.

THE GARMENT'S DESIGN

The design of the garment itself is influenced by Japanese patterns. "I was always inspired by Japanese patterns mainly because they're very artsy and they bring us back to nature… it totally reminds me of Earth and nature." The garment looks like a clear garment with green dots. It is extremely fashion forward and would complement any outfit perfectly, but Aghighi does not want the focus to be on the fashion aspect. "I wanted the focus to be about what this technology can do… What are the other qualities of the textile that are more important?" Biogarmentry is more than a fashionable piece in our closets—this concept will revolutionize the way we think about our clothing.

Seeing the effect that one's care has on the garment produces a visual result that acknowledges a greater connection. "So it creates an emotional attachment when you can actually visually see something is living… and then it starts growing and you can actually visually see it, it's just way more effective than just telling you that, hey, this thing here is alive." Knowing the garment is alive and reliant on our care creates a symbiotic relationship between the garment and the wearer. We care for the garment while it provides us protection and produces oxygen.

The garment is also affected by the care you give. "The lifespan of the textile is absolutely dependent on how you care for it, so if you take better care for it, it's going to last you a long time." Biogarmentry is meant to be a compostable so, once the algae have gone through their lifecycle, the garment can be composted.

CHANGING OUR RELATIONSHIP WITH OUR CLOTHING

Nowadays, we do not really think about the clothes we wear. At a surface level, it's just about taking that Outfit of the Day picture or just what we do to get ready during the day. "The only time that we think about clothing is the first 10 minutes in the morning that we put [them] on and then… until you, I don't know, spill some coffee on them or something happens—you don't really notice." Our clothes become an afterthought once we get ready. We don't think too much about them unless something happens to ruin them.

Our clothing should not be an afterthought. It is essentially our second skin. "This is the most intimate piece around us that's constantly with us. It's the closest thing on our body, which is the most precious thing." As our body is precious, we should be giving it more attention. What goes into making what goes onto our body, how do we care for these clothes, and how do we dispose of them? By forming an emotional connection to the garment, we can learn to become more cognizant of the environment around us, including the clothing that touches our skin.

Designers need to redesign the approach behind creating garments for consumers. "[As] designers, we have a lot more responsibility... because we create the demand before the demand is actually out there. We are the people who are telling people... what the consumers want to consume... how to consume." Designers are the ultimate influencers when it comes to setting the precedent for what to wear. If designers put more effort into creating their designs with the sustainability in mind, this will sway the mindset of the consumer as well.

The future of fashion and sustainability will be shaped by our attitudes towards both the environment and what we wear. If our garments have an added layer of care, this will shift our attention to the lifecycle of our clothes. We will start thinking about what will happen to them and what affect they will have on the environment as a whole.

This concept forces us to think about our clothing as more than just a quick, ten-minute decision in the morning. This garment requires our care and attention throughout its entire lifecycle. From designing it, to properly caring for it, to composting it, we are responsible for it.

CHAPTER 8

CHIP[S] BOARD- MAKING A FASHION STATEMENT WITH FRIES

Fries, or, as they call it in the United Kingdom, "chips" are a favorite savory snack. What happens to the potato waste that is left behind? UK based company Chip[s] Board decided to put the potato waste stream to use, creating a bioplastic called Parblex™, which has been used to create eyeglasses and buttons for both cushions and clothing.

Chip[s] Board initially started out as a group of design students looking for a way to create an alternative to Medium-Density Fiberboard (MDF) and chipboard using potatoes, which also inspired the company name. Chip[s] Board is a pun. The original product was a chipboard made from chips. The square brackets around the 's' hold their own significance as well. "It's chipboard with the S for chips, and also it's the sustainability within chipboard," says Co-founder and Chief Marketing Officer Rob Nicoll.

Rowan Minkley is Robert's co-founder and CEO of the company. It all started with a fascination with potatoes. "I was very interested to see what the humble potato could be… Rowan was working as a chef whilst at university. [The chefs] made their own chips in the kitchen, and he had access to a huge amount of potato peelings." Their access to this resource made potato waste the perfect contender for designing an alternative material. The next step was experimentation.

Like other biofabrication companies, Chip[s] Board began with the goal of providing a solution for the negative effects that traditional design materials like MDF and chipboard have on the environment. "MDF, acrylics, blue foams, all of these materials are wonderful in terms of the job they do, but obviously [they are made of] the big 10 formaldehyde and petrochemicals."

THE ENVIRONMENTAL IMPACT

According to an article published in *Slate* titled "The Eco Perils of Cheap Decor," at 0.1 parts per million, formaldehyde can cause our eyes to water and irritate our respiratory system.[77] The amount of formaldehyde found in MDF is above that. The EPA reports that homes with wood created from materials like MDF and particle board contain 0.3 parts per million, making it probable the levels of formaldehyde the wood emits has a direct impact on our health.[77] We must actively research and use materials that are sustainable and

---

77 Nina Shen Rastogi, "The Eco-Perils of Cheap Décor," *Slate,* September 15, 2009.

environmentally friendly because those materials ultimately impact our health. The resources we choose to make designs and clothing go back to the environment, and the environment affects us.

THE BEGINNINGS OF CHIP[S] BOARD

Although Robert and Rowan were graphic design students with little scientific background, their desire to find suitable alternatives to MDF and chipboard encouraged them to experiment. "There's been a really amazing path that came from that desire to one experiment, which we still have because that's who we are naturally, but also the desire to find alternatives to materials that we want to use, but don't want to keep wasting." That is the essence of biofabrication in the fashion world—creating alternatives to harmful materials through experimentation by using the biological resources and processes nature already provides.

They started doing little experiments to find some solution to their problem, "...specifically looking at starch plastics, which you can use tinned, starch, glycerin and vinegar to make a starchy film, which is really well documented as sort of a children's science experiment you can do at home." After much experimentation, Minkley and Nicoll were able to develop a chipboard with the potato waste. "It was just through that experimentation, giving our own nuance to the various methods and questioning and changing things, that we developed a material nothing like the product we have now but rather an alternative to MDF and chip board." Creating a chipboard alternative was only the beginning.

While the initial aim was to create a sustainable alternative to chipboard, the company has shifted its focus to other possibilities with potato waste. "Through iterations bringing on various amazing chemists and people in our R&D team, we've landed on a thermoplastic by sustainable, responsible bioplastic, which can be injection, molded, and extruded." Their bioplastic is called Parblex, and it closely resembles the properties of traditional plastic.

PARBLEX

When it comes to performance, measuring Parblex is difficult in comparison to every single plastic. Different plastics are catered toward their end function. Parblex's performance as a plastic also cannot be measured just by trying to snap a square sample of it. "If I gave someone my iPhone, they wouldn't try and snap it because they know they shouldn't, but if you give them a square sample, they'll try with everything to test its strength. Most people could snap a coat hanger because it is plastic, but it works perfectly." The performance of a plastic is not measured by one's ability to snap or not snap it, but by whether it fulfills its job as the desired product… which Parblex does.

Parblex is being used to create eyewear for Ace and Tate. Designer Isabel Fletcher used Parblex for her project Offcut One, which uses discarded materials like British wool, hemp linen and bamboo.[78] Her designs include colorful coats and dresses featuring buttons created from Parblex.[78] Parblex is not only the button material of choice for clothing, but

---

78 "Offcut One," Isabel Fletcher (website), accessed June 3, 2020.

Chip[s] Board also develops cushion buttons with Parblex. It's easy to forget the little things on our clothing, accessories, and furniture that are made of plastic. While they seem little to us, these things add up. While we research methods for creating alternative materials, we need to direct our efforts to little things, too.

A wide range of plastics and Parblex can be created to match the desired qualities. "You can change properties of Parblex based on adding additives, obviously making sure that those additives are as sustainable as they can be." As an alternative for plastics, Parblex eliminates the negative environmental impact that traditional plastic creates. "We massively cut down on the carbon needed to produce Parblex compared to traditional plastics… Parblex could make a huge impact if a company fully swapped to using our materials over traditional petrochemical plastics." The creation of Parblex not only uses sustainable resources; it also has a smaller carbon footprint. CO_2 is a major contributor to greenhouse gas emissions, and if companies make a complete swap from petrochemical plastics to bioplastics like Parblex, then they could remove that major negative impact.

THE CIRCULAR ECONOMY

The way Chip[s] Board creates Parblex promotes the idea of the circular economy. Their potato waste supplier is McCain, which is one of the largest potato suppliers, globally. McCain produces a lot of byproducts from their potato processing, like the flesh and the peels of the potatoes. Typically, this waste would be sent to farms to be used as low grade feed for the animals. "For the volume of that waste, actually, there's very little nutrients within that. So, it goes to bulking animal feed for commercial farming. What we do is we actually intersect that." Chip[s] Board interrupts the traditional system and introduces a better one—one that not only creates a more sustainable alternative to traditional plastic, but also one that creates better feed for animals.

In Chip[s] Board's new and improved system, the company takes the usable parts of the waste stream provided by McCain to create Parblex. What happens to the unusable part? Well, luckily, the parts of the waste they do not use can be fed to animals. "Everything we don't need is still useful as animal feed… it is actually pure and more nutrient rich because we've refined it." With their company model, Chip[s] Board produces a viable solution for two different realms: the realm of design and the realm of the food and farming industry.

Chip[s] Board further promotes the idea of a circular economy by exploring the biodegradability potential of Parblex. "It is biodegradable, compostable and recyclable." While Parblex is biodegradable, it might not meet our expectations. When we think of biodegradability, we think of composting in our backyards, the compost magically disappearing in a few weeks. Biodegradability has a large scope, though, and it does not typically translate to our thoughts on the idea.

For Parblex to be properly disposed, it needs to be industrially composted. In contrast to the traditional composting at home, industrial composting speeds up the biodegradation of a product by adding heat and moisture. The important part of ensuring the proper disposal of the bioplastic is to ensure it ends up in the right place. We have regulations in place to check this. "Currently bioplastics, if they went into plastic recycling, would be seen as a contaminant. We're looking to see how legislation will allow people to handle bio plastics in the correct way." Biofabrication of bioplastics is a relatively new field that will replace traditional plastic, so countries should put regulations into place that will ensure their disposal is treated accordingly. If we are to revolutionize the materials to become more sustainable, we need to ensure that the proper methods to dispose of that material are in place.

CHALLENGES AND MOVING FORWARD

Like any other startup, Chip[s] Board faces challenges with finding funding to scaling up. Their amazing idea and products allowed them to win initial funding and support through competitions in the UK. While this initial funding allowed them to develop their idea, they need more investment. If we want more fashion companies to invest in sustainable materials, we, the consumers, must demand it. A large demand will compel fashion companies to invest in the resources.

The ultimate goal is a complete shift to more sustainable materials in the fashion industry—making these materials the norm. Nicoll believes this will happen when using Parblex is no longer a point of interest. "So actually, the pinnacle of success for [us] would be when our materials are no longer considered interesting or noteworthy. Obviously, we'd always hope they are interesting to people… but to the industry, if they became standard, that'd be the pinnacle of what we could achieve." Parblex as the standard would shift expectations for the fashion industry, incentivizing companies to use sustainable material. Sustainability could become a requirement for the fashion industry, and that is a point for which we should reach.

PART 3

FASHIONABLE FIBERS

When it comes to the fibers that make up our clothing, we have two possibilities: either they are created from synthetic material, or they are created from natural fibers. As we have already discussed, the effects of both synthetic and natural fibers in the current fashion industry, especially common practices of creating textiles, pollutes our water sources as well as generates a large amount of carbon emissions. The World Economic Forum (WEF) reports that washing clothes with plastic-based fibers releases 500,000 tons of microfibers into the ocean, which is the equivalent of fifty billion plastic bottles.[79]

---

79 Morgan McFall-Johnsen, "These Facts Show How Unsustainable the Fashion Industry Is," *World Economic Forum,* January 21, 2020.

What we typically think is the better, more sustainable route would be to use natural fibers. Even the way the fashion industry monitors the production of natural fibers, however, uses a lot of resources and produces a lot of CO_2 emissions. The WEF reports that the fashion industry is responsible for 10% of carbon emissions produced by humans.[79]

One source of these carbon emissions, the production of wool, requires a lot of land to farm sheep. According to a study conducted by Oxford University, farming large amounts of animals on one area of land leads to the formation of heavily eroded, barren plots.[80] In addition, PETA explains that natural fibers like fur should not be defined as "natural" because they are preserved with chemicals such as ammonia, formaldehyde, hydrogen peroxide, chromates and other bleaching agents. Once again, biofabrication provides an alternative. Companies such as AlgiKnit, SmartFiber, and Piñatex propose alternative fibers, mixing the idea of the natural and synthetic to create the sustainable.

80   "Wool, Fur, and Leather: Hazardous to the Environment," *PETA*, accessed June 13, 2020.

CHAPTER 9

ALGIKNIT- CREATING KNITWEAR WITH KELP

When we think of seaweed, a few things come to mind: sushi, water, and, if you are a botanist, algae. At least for me, sweaters are not what initially come to mind. AlgiKnit is one company challenging this thought by creating fibers with seaweed.

AlgiKnit came out of a project called Bioesters, which won first place at the first BioDesign Challenge in 2016.[81] The BioDesign Challenge is a competition for scientists, designers, and artists at the high school and university level to create a project using biotechnology. These projects can range anywhere from medicine, architecture, food, energy, and, of course, fashion. Bioesters was a project created by three students from the Fashion Institute of Technology (FIT): Tessa Callaghan, Gian Cui, and Aleksandra Gosiewski, and one student from the Pratt Institute, CEO Aaron Nesser.[81] Their

---

81 "FIT Team Wins Biodesign Challenge," *FIT Newsroom,* last modified June 30, 2016.

mentors for this project were FIT professors Theanne Schiros and Asta Skocir.[81]

Together, they worked on creating fibers for knitwear, the field in which they were most familiar. They created a fiber out of a biopolymer known as alginate. According to an article published in *Process in Polymer Science* titled "Alginate: Properties and biomedical applications," alginate is an anionic, or negatively charged, polymer typically found in brown seaweed.[82]

Initially, they started experimenting with materials that other biomaterial scientists had worked with like bacterial cellulose. With the cellulose, they grew a sheet and cut it into a tank top. The bacterial cellulose did not have the right qualities, though. After doing more research, they found kelp. They combined kelp with other organic compounds and created several gels. The gels produced favorable qualities: the mix was malleable and easy to work with, creating thin films.

In an interview with *Knitting Industry Creative,* Skocir described the approach they took to test the different gels. "Being a knitwear designer, I tried different techniques like embossing it with a knit pattern to create a more interesting material and cutting it into continuous strips so it could be knit."[83] They were unable to create clothing with the films because the gel wouldn't hold together, causing the textile to fall apart.

---

82 Kuen Yong Lee and David J Mooney, "Alginate properties and biomedical applications," *Progress in polymer science* 37, no. 1 (2012): 106-126.

83 Wendy Friedman, "In Conversation with Asta Skocir, Co-Founder of AlgiKnit," *Knitting Industry Creative,* February 22, 2018.

"So, we looked further into textiles, and realized they are actually made up of yarns and fibers," Gosiewski explained at a talk she gave at Design Indaba.[84] This insight propelled the team to make the material into a yarn. Gosiewski described the first few samples as resembling 'dried ramen noodles.'[84] She explained, 'They had no structural integrity and completely fell apart.'[84]

Despite the initial makeup of the samples, they persisted, and were able to create both thick and thin yarns. "We went from dried ramen noodles to a material that actually worked."[84] They knit a tank top with this new material and saw potential for it in other aspects as well, like foams and three-dimensional printed structures. The knitted tank top was displayed at TED x FIT in October, 2017.

Schiros wore the top while giving her TED talk "BioDesign: The (R)evolution of Sustainable Fashion." Schiros gives a break-down of the process. "So, we start with seaweed. We extract a biopolymer called alginate in a powdered form, which we can then turn into a hydrogel and, using a variety of different methods, we can cast it into a thick film or extrude it into a fiber… the paste is extruded into a curing bath where chemicals crosslink the polymer chains into long fibers suitable for the textile. The only byproduct is NaCl, or table salt."[85] The fiber produced matches the qualities of a single synthetic fiber, or a single thread from your sweater.

---

84 *Design Indaba,* "Aleksandra Gosiewski talks seaweed fashion and the next stage of biotech," April 19, 2020, video, 6:53.

85 *TED,* "BioDesign: The {R}evolution of Sustainable Fashion | Theanne Schiros | TEDxFIT," Janruary 4, 2018, video, 17:55.

WHY ALGAE?

The groups chose kelp because of the many benefits of algae. Kelp is one of the fastest growing organisms; it grows two feet per day.[85] It is a huge sink for CO_2 emissions, which means that it removes the CO_2 from the atmosphere and turns it into biomass. In addition to managing the carbon emissions in the atmosphere, kelp also increases biodiversity underwater in areas that have experienced coral bleaching, ocean acidification, and other detriments due to climate change.[85] With all these amazing properties, kelp is the perfect candidate for creating textiles.

What allowed the team to create a cloth that didn't fall apart was returning to what fashion is familiar with when it comes to creating textiles: fibers. What's incredible about this process is that no harmful byproducts are produced when creating the fibers. The only byproduct is table salt, which is edible and definitely not like the toxic waste thrown out by factories today. Imagine the fashion industry adopting this method of production. Not only will we have more fashion forward fibers, we will also get seasoning for our food. This is the perfect example of the circular economy, which aims to eliminate the waste produce and instead create a byproduct that can be used elsewhere.

When it comes to dyeing the fibers, the bioyarn created from the kelp can be dyed using natural pigments. The AlgiKnit team experimented with natural dyes like cochineal, marigold, and even compost, which all have no trouble binding to the fiber. "What's very exciting about this is that we can incorporate the color directly into the paste before extrusion or casting of the films, eliminating the water use and emissions of dip dyeing practices."[85] Through seeking out natural methods of dyeing, AlgiKnit not only eliminates the unnecessary amount of waste produced from creating fibers, they also show the potential of using fewer resources in the dyeing industry as well.

This proves the fashion industry does have avenues through which they can change their current practices. These sustainable options for both dyeing and creating textiles in ways that produce little to no waste, or even produce a useful byproduct are available. We just need to pull them into the mainstream fashion industry.

GOING BEYOND KNITWEAR

Textiles and fibers are not the only product on which AlgiKnit is working. They have also been working on their own line of shoes called AlgiKicks. This shoe has three layers. The first layer is a knit textile, the insole is a foam sheet, and the outsole is a 3D printed lattice. Gosiewski says "The beauty of this product is that when it is worn out, or you no longer want it, it can be broken down by microorganisms, and the nutrients can be reclaimed to feed the next generation of product."[86]

This is the advantage of the circular economy. Through this means of production, rather than destroying the environment around us, we develop a symbiotic relationship with it. The environment provides us with the resources we need

---

86 *Design Indaba,* "Aleksandra Gosiewski talks seaweed fashion and the next stage of biotech," April 19, 2020, video, 6:53.

to make our materials, and we, rather than produce harmful waste, create food for the microorganisms they can generate more product for us.

AlgiKnit's endeavors were funded through investments and different competitions. They received the Chasing Genius Award from *National Geographic,* which awarded them $25,000.[87] According to *SynBioBeta,* in 2018, Horizon Ventures invested $2.2 million dollars into AlgiKnit.[88] Horizon Ventures is a private investment company that also invested in big companies such as Facebook and Spotify. This is huge for AlgiKnit and the development of biomaterials. Many start-up biomaterial companies are unable to further their research or go beyond the idea stage due to lack of funding. With this investment, hopefully AlgiKnit will be amongst the fibers that makeup our everyday clothes.

The future of the apparel industry is not going to look like what we think of today. Fast fashion cannot continue to rule our closets. When it comes to sustainable textiles, AlgiKnit demonstrates the potential of using kelp as a reliable fiber. When it comes to creating apparel, tank tops or shoes, we could bury them in the ground and be benefiting the eco-system for a change. Schiros contrasts the models of creation from designers and scientists to nature. "Scientists tend to look at materials from the molecule up, but designers have a different approach—from the top down, thinking of construction. But nature, nature looks at materials from every

---

87 "AlgiKnit Wins a National Geographic Chasing Genius Award," *FIT Newsroom,* last modified September 18, 2017.

88 "AlgiKnit Closes $2.2M Seed Round to Develop Kelp-Derived Yarn," *SynBioBeta,* las modified November 16, 2018.

direction. Nature makes exactly what it needs and doesn't waste a thing—complete recycling of matter and energy. The byproducts of one reaction are the feed stop for the next."[89]

Nature knows what she's doing, and she can teach us a thing or two, especially when it comes to creating materials. Hopefully, by further studying and paying attention to the way in which nature recycles, creates, and recreates, we can learn to implement the beneficial phenomena we observe and integrate them into how we produce clothing.

---

89 *TED,* "BioDesign: The {R}evolution of Sustainable Fashion | Theanne Schiros | TEDxFIT," Janruary 4, 2018, video, 17:55.

CHAPTER 10

SMARTFIBER AG- FIBERS FOR OUR SKIN

———

Kelp is not the only marine life that has been used to create fibers; their close relative, seaweed, is another great contender for creating fibers. Beyond just the benefits that algae like kelp and seaweed provide to underwater ecosystems, they provide benefits to us as well. Seaweed contains more vitamins, minerals, and trace elements compared to any other natural organism in the world.[90]

A journal article published in *Mar Drugs* titled "Beneficial Effects of Marine Algae-Derived Carbohydrates for skin Health," states that different types of algae such as red, green, and brown have all been found to have properties associated with anti-aging, anti-inflammation, and anti-skin cancer properties, as well as properties that promote dermal tissue

———

90 "SeaCell™: The natural fiber with the skin-caring properties of pure seaweed," *smartfiberAG newsroom* (blog), September 18, 2014, accessed June 1, 2020.

production.[91] When we think about the type of materials that make up our clothing, we should realize that what interacts most with this clothing is us, our skin. When it comes to skincare, we try to purchase the products that are most beneficial for our skin, and we should have the same approach when it comes to the clothes that cover our skin. SmartFiber AG is a company headquartered in Rudolstadt, Germany, and founded in 2005. SmartFiber AG uses seaweed to create textile fibers known as SeaCell™ and has been doing so for more than a decade. Like AlgiKnit, SmartFiber uses brown seaweed, specifically *Ascophyllum nodosum*.[90] The common names for this species of seaweed are rockweed and knotted kelp, and it is found near the fjords of Iceland.[90]

SEAWEED AS A FIBER

These amazing properties of seaweed translate to SeaCell™. A test conducted by Intertek, a product testing and certification company, found that fabrics containing just 24 percent of SeaCell™ fibers catch 91 percent of free radicals when exposed to them.[92] According to an article published in the *International Journal of Biomedical Science,* a free radical is a molecule that has one or more unpaired electrons in its outermost shell.[93] They can cause cells to go into oxidative stress, meaning the cell cannot destroy the free radical.[93] During oxidative stress, free radicals can damage DNA.[93]

---

91 Ji Hye Kim et al., "Beneficial Effects of Marine Algae-Derived Carbohydrates for Skin Health," *Marine Drugs* 16, no. 11 (2018): 459.

92 "New confirmation to take care of antioxidantien on our skin with our SeaCell™ fiber," *smartfiber AG* (blog), March 9, 2019, accessed June 1, 2020.

93 Lien Ai Pharm-Huy et al., "Free Radicals, Antioxidants in Disease and Health," *International Journal of Biomedical Science* 4, no. 2 (2008): 89-96.

For example, they form hydroxylated bases, which interfere with normal cell growth and gene transcription.[94] Oxidative stress is also linked to cancer and arthritis, as well as auto-immune, cardiovascular, and neurodegenerative diseases.[94] When we think of fibers nowadays, we don't acknowledge the protection they can provide for us. With this test, SeaCell™ protects the skin at the cellular and molecular level. Fibers with this ability both protect and heal our skin.

The use of natural fibers is not a completely new idea. Native Americans used natural fibers to weave together textiles. While the companies of today are not using the finger weaving methods of Native Americans to construct textiles, companies like AlgiKnit and SmartFiber are creating fibers from kelp and seaweed. This is similar to how Native Americans used plant fibers as materials to create their garments and textiles. Seaweed has many properties that are beneficial to human skin. It has substances that aid in cell regeneration and is high in antioxidants. Naturally, these properties make the perfect qualities for textiles. We don't have to return to the exact practices of textile making of Native Americans, but we can learn to borrow their techniques and ideas to create more sustainable practices for the future.

A FIBER FOR SENSITIVE SKIN

SmartFiber not only created a fiber using the healing properties of seaweed, they also created a fiber with zinc oxide known as smartcel™ sensitive. This oxide is specifically designed for people that have sensitive skin or suffer from

---

94 Ibid.

skin conditions such as eczema or neurodermitis. Zinc Oxide is a common ingredient in sunscreens. A study published in the *Journal of the European Academy of Dermatology and Venereology* titled "Skin benefits from continuous topical administration of akin oxide/petrolatum formulation by a novel disposable diaper" looked at the effect that a zinc oxide ointment would have if put in children's diapers.[95] The control group's diapers had no zinc oxide/petrolatum, and the experimental group's diapers had zinc oxide/petrolatum.[95] The study found that wearing the diaper with the zinc oxide/petrolatum significantly reduced diaper rash and skin erythema.[95] Skin erythema refers to the redness of the skin. If zinc oxide has the potential to reduce rashes when added as an ointment in children's diapers, then it should also have this same ability when applied to textiles.

The healing properties of smartcel™ sensitive were tested in a study published in the journal *Cosmetic Medicine* in a paper titled "Clinical experiences with an antimicrobial bed equipment using zinc smartcel™ fibers for pronounced atopic dermatitis." In the study, ten patients between the ages of 18 to 74 years old were examined over a period of ten to twelve days.[96] They were assessed on three different parameters: neurodermatitis severity, itching intensity, and

---

95 S. Baldwin et al., "Skin Benefits from continuous topical administration of zinc oxide/petrolatum formulation by a novel disposable diaper," *Journal of The European Academy of Dermatology and Venereology* 15, no. 1 (2001): 5-11.

96 Uwe Wolina et al., "Clincal experiences with an antimicrobial bed equipment using znc-smartcell™ fibers for pronounced atopic dermatitis," *Cosmetic Medicine* 4, no. 23 (2019): 20-23.

sleeping habits.[97] These parameters were scored from before and after the smartcel™ bedding sheets were used.

The study found that after using the bedding, the patients' severity of neurodermatitis went down, the intensity of itching went down, and sleep duration increased by 1-2 hours in half of the patients. If all our textiles had these healing capabilities, this would not only transform our wardrobes, it would also transform our lifestyles. Our clothes would not just be something we wear, but something that interacts with us, benefiting our skin with its touch.

THE LYOCELL PRODUCTION PROCESS

Both smartcel™ sensitive and SeaCell™ are made through the lyocell production process. The basic idea of lyocell production is to process the pulp from wood in a closed loop without altering any chemicals. In the closed loop process, the chemicals generated in the process are reused as solvent during the production of fiber. Both smartcel™ sensitive and SeaCell™ are produced with Lenzing AG in Austria. The lyocell process is an environmentally friendly process, and it consists of five steps: dissolution, filtration, spinning regeneration, washing, and finishing.[7]

Dissolution involves breaking apart the seaweed fibers and mixing it into a solution continuing cellulose and a compound known as N-methyl morpholine-N-oxide (NMMO) to form a thicker liquid.[98] In the filtration step, the thick liquid

---

97 Ibid.

98 Shokai Zheng etal., "Regenetated Cellulose by the Lyocell Process, a Brief Review of the Process and Properties," *BioResources* 12, no. 2 (2018):

is filtered to get rid of the extra, rough elements. During spinning regeneration, the thick liquid is forced through a spinneret and placed in a bath where it regenerates through coagulation.[98] At this point the lyocell fibers have formed. In the washing phase, these fibers are washed and the NMMO compound is recovered and recycled for later use.[98] Finally, the finishing phase involves dyeing the product and preparing it for use in textiles.[98] The difference between the two fibers is in the materials that go into making them. smartcel™ sensitive is made from a mixture of recycled zinc that oxidized into a white powder forming zinc oxide.[98]

SmartFiber produces fibers that are not only sustainable, but also have healing properties. A study has already shown their fiber's ability to help patients with their sleep patterns as well as their skin conditions. With fibers like this, the application can go beyond fashion and help in the medical world as well, whether that is creating bed sheets or super soft socks. For everyday wear, we will have a completely different relationship with our clothing. It will go beyond just something that we wear to express ourselves, and we will become more aware of the relationship our skin has with the fibers that it touches. When we are more conscious about what goes into making our clothing, we are not only creating sustainable practice for our planet, we are taking care of ourselves too.

4577-4592.

CHAPTER 11

ANANAS ANAM AND PIÑATEX

Pineapples are not just a refreshing summer fruit or controversial pizza topping; they have also made their debut in the fashion world. Imagine telling your friends your coat is made from pineapple leaves! That sounds pretty cool to me!

Ananas Anam is a London-based company looking at sustainability not only in terms of environmental impact, but also in terms of the ethical implications. Piñatex is a textile made up of fibers from pineapple leaves and is meant present an alternative to leather. These pineapple leaves are harvested from farming communities in the Philippines and allow farmers to create an additional income.[99] Piñatex is a textile that is both socially and environmentally responsible.[99]

---

99   "About us," Piñatex, accessed June 11, 2020.

THE BEGINNINGS OF PIÑATEX

The development of Piñatex began with Dr. Carmen Hijosa, who was consulting on the leather export industry of the Philippines in the 1990s.[99] While she was learning more about the leather export industry, she was shocked to find the negative impact leather production and chemical tanning had on the environment.[99]

One aspect of the leather making process is tanning the hide to prevent it from decomposing. Tanning is an extensive process that requires 250 chemicals, which include toxins like hexavalent chromium, aldehyde, cyanide, zinc, and lead. According to the United States Department of Labor, hexavalent chromium is known to cause cancer, and it affects the respiratory system, kidneys, liver, skin, and eyes.[100]

Hijosa, aware of the environmental impact of traditional animal leather processing, was determined to find an alternative. Two alternatives to traditional leather are synthetic leathers: one made from polyurethane and another made from polyvinyl fiber (PVC). Polyurethane is made from fossil fuels and PVC is just another form of plastic. Neither of these alternatives present a sustainable option for an alternative to leather.

In addition to the environmental implications of tanning leather, the textile industry has unethical labor practices. In the current textile industry, the supply chain is so complicated that pinpointing the unethical employment practices of the industry, specifically child labor, is difficult. Reports from

---

100 "Hexavalent Chromium," United States Department of Labor, accessed June 11, 2020.

the Centre for Research on Multinational Corporations and the Indian Committee of the Netherlands from 2014 indicate that workers in the textile industry work in "appalling conditions that amount to modern day slavery and the worst forms of child labour."[101]

CREATING A MORE SUSTAINABLE AND ETHICAL FASHION INDUSTRY

When we think about a more sustainable fashion industry, we should be considering it on two fronts—an environmental perspective as well as a social perspective. "We always say that sustainability is not only about environment, it's also about society. So that that is a strong point in our development," says Dr. Raquel Prado, the sustainability and research manager for the company. With Ananas Anam's model, sustainable is defined as not only providing a more eco-friendly textile alternative, but also being socially responsible for the means through which the textile is created.

WEAVING IN THE PHILIPPINES

While Hijosa was in the Philippines, she noticed the locals were weaving garments with pineapple leave fibers. According to the Philippine Folklife Museum, to obtain the fiber, the leaves are cut from the pineapple plant.[102] Fibers can be classified into three different groups: *liniwan*, *bastos*, and *pininupok*.[102] *Liniwan* is the finest of the three fibers and is

---

101 Josephine Moulds, "Child labour in the fashion supply chain," *The Guardian*, n. d.

102 "History and Origin of Piña," Philippine Folklife Museum Foundation, accessed June 11, 2020.

used to weave the desired textile.[102] *Bastos* is a coarse fiber and is used to make twine.[102] *Pininupok* is also a fine fiber.[102] The fibers are split from the leaves.[102] Each fiber is knotted to create one continuous fiber.[102] The fibers are combed and washed in the river to clean and brighten them.[102]

These fibers are then hand-woven into *barong tagalong,* wedding dresses, formal dresses, table cloths, bags, and other items.[103] The *barong tagalong* is an embroidered long sleeve t-shirt for men and the national dress of the Philippines.[103] Learning about the traditional methods of creating textiles from pineapple leaf fibers, Hijosa found a sustainable alternative to creating leather, which led to the development of Piñatex.[104]

PIÑATEX TODAY

The fibers for Piñatex come from pineapple harvesting farms in the Philippines. The pineapple leaves are typically a byproduct and considered agricultural waste. With the model the company has in place, they use this byproduct for fiber creation. "Pineapple harvesting is 18 months… but in between plantation or even between harvesting, they have no income." With Ananas Anam, farmers can make an additional income making fibers during the off-season.

LIFE CYCLE

The life cycle of the Piñatex textile can be divided into eight steps: leaf collection, fiber extraction, washing and drying,

---

103 "History of the Barong Tagalog," My Barong, accessed June 11, 2020.
104 "About us," Piñatex, accessed June 11, 2020.

purification, piñafelt, coating, finishing, and creating the end product.[105] During extraction, semi-automatic machines extract long fibers from the pineapple leaves.[105] Fibers are washed, then dried naturally in the sun.[105] Then, the pineapple leaf fiber (PALF) is mixed with polylactic acid (PLA) to create a non-woven mesh called piñafelt.[105] Rolls of piñafelt are shipped to from the Philippines to Spain or Italy for finishing, and then it can be used to create any product from garments to accessories.[105]

PIGMENTATION VS TRADITIONAL DYEING

Piñatex's coloring does not come from dyeing the textile but from pigmentation. The company uses the most sustainable options to color the textile. Prado explains this pigmentation process. She says, "We do pigmentation so the pigment is dispersed in the resin, and then applied to a coating. We really focus on the fact that we need to use certified pigments that are in tune with regulations, and they are not polluting. We are always looking for the most sustainable option that the market has."

Prado further explains that coloring Piñatex using pigmentation, rather than dyeing, uses less water. "We need to apply that coating anyway… so we don't need this extra step of value, so we are saving water in the process." In traditional textile dyeing, a dye bath is created to dye textiles. According to an article published in *Fashion Revolution,* 200 tons of water per ton of fabric are used in the dyeing process. By

---

105 Ibid.

dispersing pigment in the textile, the need to use water for a dye bath is completely eliminated.[106]

BIODEGRADABILITY OF PIÑATEX

Strong discussions around the biodegradability of the Piñatex textile occur today. As I mentioned earlier with Chip[s] Board's bioplastic Parblex, the term biodegradability has a wide scope of meaning. When we think of this word, we automatically associate it with composting in our backyard. In this case, it would take a very long time. In order for Piñatex to be properly composted, it would need to be industrially composted. As the fashion world shifts more toward biomaterials, proper protocol for their disposal will need to be established. For example, companies will need to create an industrial composting plant and properly label products to explain how a consumer should dispose of them, like they do with recycling.

THE FUTURE

Like many other startups, the most challenging part for Ananas Anam has been funding for scaling up production. As more biotech companies come into the sphere of fashion, it is important to invest in the work they are doing so there can be more research done to improve upon their findings. Currently, Ananas Anam is working to create a more biobased coating for the Piñatex textile. Currently, the coating is polyurethane, which is a plastic base. This base makes up 10

---

106 Beth Ranson, "The true cost of colour: the impact of textile dyes on water systems," *Fashion Revolution*, February 13, 2020.

percent of the fabric. The ultimate goal is to completely eliminate the plastic-based PU coating and create an eco-friendly, bio-based one. This would also require more research and funding.

The Piñatex textile has already found its place in the mainstream fashion world, creating items from outerwear to shoes and everything in between. Designer Miriam Al Sibai used the Piñatex textile in the shade Paprika Pluma, which is a bright red-orange, to create outwear for her company. "The texture is interesting. Although it may appear to look like cow leather, it doesn't feel the same and is unique to leather," she says, "It is such a gorgeous fabric to work with and its structured aesthetic has been great for our coats."[107] Piñatex also did a collaboration with H&M on their conscious collection in 2019.[107]

Already breaking into the fashion industry, the Piñatex textile is surely a strong alternative to leather. Ananas Anam hopes to educate both consumers and designers alike about making the most sustainable choice when it comes to purchasing materials and our clothes. "It's kind of an education of the consumer, so we need to change bit by bit," says Prado.

Let's make it fashionable to know what goes into making your favorite red overcoat. Let's make it fashionable to choose the more sustainable option. So as consumers, let's try to educate ourselves and make that choice.

---

107 "/#Made from Piñatex," Products, Piñatex, accessed June 11, 2020.

PART 4

BACTERIA TO DYE FOR

Think about your favorite red dress. What went into making it this ravishing red color? Apparently, a lot more than you would expect. According to the World Resources Institute, globally, the fashion industry uses 1.3 trillion gallons of water every year for dyeing fabric.[108] Not only does the textile industry use large amounts of water, it also damages the natural environments of the developing countries where these factories are located.

Bangladesh is one country that is home to some of these factories. In Bangladesh, the textile industry constitutes 82 percent of the country's exports earnings.[109] In 2016, the

---

108 Deborah Drew and Genevieve Yehounme, "The Apparel Industry's Environmental Impact Impact in 6 Graphics," *World Resources Institute* (blog), July 5, 2017.

country produced 217 million tons of water waste, and is projected to produce 349 million tons in 2021.[109] According to the National Resources Defense Council, the four rivers in Dhaka, the capital of Bangladesh, are considered ecologically critical due to industrial and textile waste.[110]

That's a lot of water and a lot of damage to the environment to bring a little pop of color into our wardrobes. While the industry's current means for dyeing fabric grossly misuses natural resources, our closets should not be devoid of color. Luckily, Biology has presented an alternative means: bacteria.

Bacteria dyes fabric? Sounds a little weird, I know. Trust me, if you want to be fashion forward in the next few seasons to come, you will be wearing clothing dyed by bacteria. Where can you find such attire, you may ask? Well, some companies are working on projects to create methods to keep you fashion enthusiasts eco-friendly and on top of the current trends. Companies like Faber Futures, Vienna Textile Lab, Living Colour, and Huue hope to color our closets by working with bacteria.

109 Laila Hossain, Sumit Kanto Sarker, and Mohidus Samad Khan, "Evalution of present and future wastewater impacts impacts of textile dyeing industries in Bangladesh," *Environmental Development* 26, (2018): 23-33.

110 Standout Practices at High-Performing Bangladeshi Textile Mills: How Top Resource-Efficient Factories in Bangladesh Save Money and Curb Pollution (NRDC), 2.

CHAPTER 12

FABER FUTURES-ADD SOME COELICOLOR TO YOUR WORLD

What would our wardrobes become if they were devoid of color? Without color, we lose a key quality of our textiles. Traditional textile dyeing uses toxic chemicals that damage our natural water sources. Bacterial dyeing, on the other hand, eliminates the use of the chemicals. Project Coelicolor explores the potential that the bacteria *Streptomyces coelicolor* has to produce dyes. *Streptomyces coelicolor* produces an antibiotic called actionrhodin, which comes in different colors such as red, blue, and pink. The color of the antibiotic is dependent on the acidity of its environment. The bacteria can be grown directly on the fabric, for example silk. This process requires only 200 millimeters of water. According to an article published in *GreenBiz,* traditional dyeing uses somewhere between 25 to 40 gallons of water for every two pounds of fabric.[111] This is 500 times more water than what is used with *Streptomyces coelicolor* as a dyeing agent.[112]

Natsai Audrey Chizea began Project Coelicolor in 2011 when Professor John Ward at the University College of London introduced her to the properties of *Streptomyces coelicolor*.[112] At the time, Ward was researching the bacteria in his lab to get a better understanding of antibiotics.[112] What Chizea found intriguing was the bacteria's ability to produce color, and this is where she saw its potential use as a tool in design.[112]

THE BACTERIA: STREPTOMYCES COELICOLOR

Streptomyces coelicolor is a bacterium that is found in the soil. According to an article published in *Nature* titled "Complete genome sequence of the model actinomycete Streptomyces coelicolor A3(2)," this is a crucial bacteria for the environment.[113] *Streptomyces coelicolor* is involved in decomposing organisms, degrading compounds such as chitin and lignocellulose.[113] In 2002, the year the paper was published, the bacteria was responsible for two thirds of naturally derived antibiotics that were in use in the medical world.[113] *Streptomyces coelicolor* provides tools for both the ecosystem as well as the medical world, so surely it can help out in the design world as well.

---

111 Lauren Phipps, "Just dye it: how this apparel company is developing water-and chemical-free textile tinting," *GreenBiz*, February 26, 2019,

112 "Project Coelicolor," The Index Project, accessed June 11, 2020.

113 S. D. Bentley et al., "Complete genome sequence of the model actinomycete *Streptomyces Coelicolor* A3(2)," *Nature* 417, (2002): 141-147.

TRADITIONAL DYEING VS BACTERIAL DYEING

According to an article published in the *American Journal of Environmental Science and Engineering* titled "Health and Environmental Impact of Dyes: Mini Review," textile dyeing not only uses a lot of water, but it also damages natural water sources as well.[114] It is estimated that for every 12 to 20 tons of textiles, 1000 to 3000 cubic meters of waste is produced, which ends up in our water sources.[4] This waste includes organic and inorganic compounds that cause health problems such as asthma, watery eyes, and itching.[114]

Dyeing with bacteria removes the need for these additional chemicals known as effluents, which help the dye stick to the fabric. In a Vimeo video discussing Project Coelicolor, Chizea says, "We are not using any chemicals to fix those pigment molecules onto the textiles. This is fascinating because any textile designer will tell you that a lot of the harm is caused in the dyeing stage because of the chemistry inputs that go into being able to create that bond between molecule and fiber."[115] With bacteria dyeing, the bacteria are grown directly on the fabric, so additional effluents to ensure a fiber to dye bond is not needed.

When it comes to using bacteria to dye fabric, one concern is the way in which to control it. "When you design with a living system… you are actively producing innovative, novel ways of manufacturing, so there's a real opportunity for innovative practice to happen with biofabrication," says

---

114 Mohamed A. Hassaan and Ahmed El Nemr, "Health and Environmental Impacts of Dyes: Mini Review," *American Journal od Environmental Science and Engineering* 1, no. 3 (2017): 64-67.

115 *The Index Project*, "Project Coelicolor," September 5, 2019, video, 03:33.

Chizea at a 2018 talk with the *Business of Fashion*, "… it's difficult because you can't control nature, and that's a beautiful thing."[116] While bacteria are living creatures, we can influence the colors and patterns they produce on fabric by controlling their environment. For example, *Streptomyces coelicolor* produces different colored pigments depending on the acidity of its environment. They can dye textiles with organic patterns, geometric patterns, as well as create a solid colored textile. The dye patterns can be influenced by "twisting, folding, clamping, dipping, spraying, and submerging."[6]

PATTERNS AND TEXTURE

Chizea explains the texture of the final result of the color demonstrates the artistry behind dyeing with *Streptomyces coelicolor*. "I look at color, and I want to know what the texture of that color is because that's how *Streptomyces* dyes uniformly. It always does it uniformly but is this beautiful three dimensionality to the effect of introducing the microbe to that fabric."[116] The patterns that the bacteria create with the dye give a tie dye effect, or they create patterns that look like the fabric has been dipped in watercolor paints. The organic pattern looks like little dots that form after a paintbrush splatters paint onto a canvas. "Organic pattern is one of our key protocols," Chizea says, "and it's a beautiful metaphor. Every single dot is a colony that lived and died for seven days."[117]

---

116 *The Business of Fashion*, "Making With Life: Design Driven Biology | Natsai Audrey Chieza, Faber Futures | #BoFVOICES 2018," May 29, 2019, video, 15:57.

117 Ibid.

FABER FUTURES AND ADDITIONAL PROJECTS

Chizea's amazing work with *Streptomyces coelicolor* eventually led her to start a biodesign agency called Faber Futures, which hopes to help biodesign companies and projects research and further their ideas to create alternative materials for the design world.

As for Project Coelicolor, Chizea has teamed up with Gingko Bioworks, a company that designs organisms—sounds pretty cool. With Gingko Bioworks, Faber Futures is working on using bioengineering to cater *Streptomyces coelicolor* creating bespoke patterns as well as increasing the scale of the production.

In her Ted Talk, "Fashion has a pollution problem—biology can fix it," Chizea describes how biology allows for a more precise method of design. She says, "Now throughout the use of synthetic biology… we can now rapidly prototype the assembly of DNA. That means we can engineer the sort of biological precision that makes it possible to design a bacterium that can recycle metal."[118] Through biology, nature has already provided a set blueprint on how to create. Nature has perfected biological systems over millennia, we just need to learn how to cater the design it has already put in place.

Faber Futures has had several projects come out of Project Coelicolor. In collaboration with Gingko Bioworks, Faber Futures created a pigment for the *Forbes* Pigment Collection.[119] This pigment was the first pigment that was labeled

---

118 Natsai Audrey Chieza, "Fashion has a pollution problem-can we fix it?" filmed October 2017 at TED@BCG Milan, Milan, Italy, video, 12:45.

119 "On the Faber Future x Ginkgo Residency," Faber Futures, April 6, 2018.

with DNA.[119] Assemblage 002 is another project—one commissioned by the Cooper Hewitt Museum.[120] It is a reversible silk coat with patterned pieces representing experiments with different growth conditions to control the bacteria's growth and production.[9] The experimental approaches used on each patch can now be recreated.

THE FUTURE

The world of textile dyeing should not continue to be based in petrochemicals. With the Industrial Revolution and our practices to increase the efficiency and scale of production, have focused mainly on the products themselves, rather than what goes into and comes out of that production. Bacteria dyeing not only produces the same result as traditional industrial practices, it also uses less resources and does not affect the environment by creating large amounts of waste water. Bacterial dyeing is the next step for textile dyeing. We need to learn how to harness the tools nature has already perfected through research and experimentation.

120 "Nature-Cooper Hewitt Design Triennial," Faber Futures, October 5, 2019.

CHAPTER 13

DESIGNING COLOR WITH BACTERIA AT VIENNA TEXTILE LAB

Color gives our textile personality. This allows us to blend into a crowd or stand out from it. As consumers and designers, we like to take control of our end product, with a specific design, pattern, or uniformity in mind. Bacteria are living organisms, so they are not so easily controlled. Maybe rather than trying to control the bacteria, we can involve them in the design process. There are many ways to create color from bacteria. At Vienna Textile Lab, bacteria create color when put under stress. For example, a bacterium is under stress when hungry. Bacteria grows in a petri dish overnight. As it grows and multiplies, it eats all the food in its medium. Once the food is all gone, the bacteria is hungry and in a state of stress. At this point, it starts producing color. "So, from one night to the other, you come in the morning and it's blue. It's amazing, I think," says Karin Fleck who is the founder of Vienna Textile Lab. Bacteria produces color overnight; that's pretty awesome.

THE BEGINNINGS

Karin Fleck is not a biotechnologist but a chemist that has always been fascinated by color. In fact, for her thesis, she explored colors: how they are used and what properties they have. Her background in chemistry lead her to start working for the oil and energy business after university or the "bad guys" as she calls them.

Unsatisfied with working with the "bad guys," Fleck took a break from her career. During her break, one of her friends from Amsterdam came to Vienna to give a talk and gave Fleck a visit. Her friend had built the Amsterdam Textile Lab, which was experimenting with how bacteria can produce color.

When her friend came to Vienna, Fleck noticed she was wearing a scarf with beautiful patterns on it. "It's dyed with bacteria," Fleck's friend informed her. This sparked Fleck's interest with the project. As a designer, her friend was struggling with upscaling and understanding how to make it work.

"Yeah, well I am a chemist," Fleck replied, "I can probably put a team together that can look into it."

A few months later, Fleck took Vienna Textile Lab and the idea of dyeing with bacteria to Austin, Austria to compete in the 2017 Climate Launchpad. Climate Launchpad is a competition that showcases businesses with environmentally friendly propositions.[121]

Preparing for the launchpad, she started assembling her team. "I got to know artists who produce the bacteria. I got to know a dye house in India that works with natural dyes." Artists and biologists are not mutually exclusive. Biologists can create art with their craft and, in the case of Vienna Textile Lab, with bacteria. Vienna Textile Lab won three awards at the competition. They won the Austrian Finals, received third place in the International Finals, and was awarded the Audience Award.

BACTERIAL DYEING

Bacterial dyeing eliminates a majority of the greenhouse gases produced during traditional textile dyeing. Compared to traditional industry dyeing, bacterial dyes use 90 percent less CO_2, 90 percent less H_2O, and 99 percent less toxic waste.[1] With this large difference, bacterial dyeing is clearly the more environmentally friendly option. So how do we use this dye color the fabric? One way is to put the fabric on the petri dish while the bacteria is growing. The bacteria grow on the fabric.

After the bacteria colors the fabric, the bacteria are killed, the fabric is washed, and this creates the product: a dyed piece of fabric.

---

121 *ClimateLaunchpad*, "Vienna Textile Lab pitch- ClimateLaunchpad Grand Finale 2017," November 15, 2017, video, 5:08.

One bacteria Vienna Textile Lab works with is called *Janth-inobacterium lividum*. *J. lividium* produces violacein, which is a bluish pigment with antimicrobial properties.[122] Antimicrobial properties are properties that allow a substance to kill bacteria, viruses, and fungi.

When it comes to dyeing fabric with bacteria, the end product creates surprising results. The bacteria have a mind of their own and are not always willing to cooperate. "They have personalities even though they are not animals, and they are not plants, so don't get me wrong… but it's like they do have personality."

Their personalities sometimes cause them to rebel. "Sometimes it can be frustrating if one decides to go on strike, and not grow anymore, but that's another story. So, you keep on talking to them, you play music, and keep a positive atmosphere." As living organisms, bacteria have a mind of their own, but this is a creative opportunity. Rather than resisting their independent nature, we can think of them as co-designers and collaborate with them to make something amazing.

With all the collaborations Vienna Textile Lab partakes in, different expectations can be discussed with the result of the dye. "We work with very different people, so we talk to really large fashion companies, we talk with textile companies, we talk with dye houses, and we work with designers and artists on all levels."

---

122 Natalia Valdes et al., "Draft genome sequence of *Janthinobacterium lividium* strain MTR reveals its mechanism of capnophilic behavior," *Standard Genomic Science*, no. 10 (2015): 110.

Fleck explains in order to create a uniformly dyed textile, they shake the dye produced from the bacteria. If this step is not done, then their "personalities" might decide to create their own patterns on the fabric. With their artistry, the bacteria manage to intrigue designers.

"We are also super proud when we don't get an even dye result, and then the designer comes into the lab, and she is really excited… and you sort of learn to let go." It seems the bacteria hope to launch their own career as designers, and they might be really successful at it.

Working with bacteria presents interesting challenges. When bacteria produce color, it does not always produce a strong color, so it needs enhancements. This can be solved with further experimentation. Fleck says, "I would say this is something I trust in science—that I will figure out." Science will take the fashion industry to new levels, but this requires time, money, and experimentation.

The dyes the bacteria create work with both natural and synthetic fibers. In the normal dyeing industry, to color fabric, dyes need mordants. A mordant is a substance that aids in the application of the dye to the textile. Mordants help dyes bind to textile. According to a paper titled "Textile dyeing industry an environmental hazard," mordants are highly toxic and negatively impact water sources when they are released as waste. Dyeing through bacteria eliminates the need for a mordant.[123]

---

123 Rita Kant, "Textile dyeing industry an environmental hazard," *Natural Science* 4, no. 1 (2012).

The bacteria dye result is different depending on the fabric. Amongst the natural fibers, bacteria dyes silk the best, and amongst the synthetic fibers, polyester produces the best dyeing result. These two fabrics produce the darkest colors. Each fiber requires a different method of enhancing the color because the chemistries of the fabrics are different. This requires experimentation and catering each dyeing process to each individual fiber.

CHALLENGES

While it may seem the switch to bacterial dyeing is the obvious choice, many challenges come with introducing it into the mainstream fashion industry—namely, the costs associated with maintaining and upscaling a startup. It's easier for investors and biotechnology professionals to get caught up in the little details, but there's a bigger picture here. If we hope to start creating a more sustainable fashion industry, we need to start by giving startups the financial resources and investments they need to start creating that impact.

Vienna Textile Lab works at the Vienna University of Technology, which allows them to better experiment with the bacteria. Upscaling, though, still poses as a cost challenge. Money is important for startup companies to mass produce their product.

Investors need to realize that this is about going beyond the little details. This is about changing the way we dye textiles in the fashion industry. "Because this is about revolution, the revolution of fashion, (or the textile industry in general) and about having a different type of production system. That is amazing." This revolution does not begin in labs, rather it begins in the mindset of us consumers.

As consumers, we should think beyond just wanting to buy a dress for its pretty color. We need to start thinking about what goes into creating that color. When Fleck gives lectures to design students, she tells them to think beyond the Pantone color they choose for the designs. "Think about the color that you use. What's behind it? Think about what natural colors you can use and think about color in a different way."

I think this goes for designers and trendsetters alike. We need to start thinking about what goes into coloring our clothing. Our purchasing choices tell businesses what we want. If we want to push towards a more sustainable way of dyeing our clothes, we need to start purchasing clothing that reflects that desire. This will cause fashion businesses and clothing companies to realize that a more sustainable means of production is the best method, and they will be more conscious of what goes into making their products.

This fashion revolution begins with us as consumers, so let's choose our colors wisely.

CHAPTER 14

BACTERIA- LITERAL LIVING COLOUR

What do sound frequencies, bacteria, color pigmentation, and fashion have to do one another? Most people would argue that these elements have nothing in common, but the founders of Living Colour disagree.

Designers Laura Luchtman and Ilfa Siebenhaar met in 2016 at a six-month long course called "Textile Academy" offered through the Waag Academy in Amsterdam. Luchtman and Siebenhaar connected while they took a workshop on pigmenting bacteria. During their workshop, they started doing research on the influence of sound frequencies on a bacteria's ability to produce color. They sought to answer the question "What effect do sound frequencies have on the growth of bacterial pigments?" More specifically, they wanted to know how to use sound to control the way bacterial pigments grow on textiles. After their month-long course ended, they decided to continue their research and called their biodesign project Living Colour.

THE SCIENCE BEHIND SOUND

Using sound to influence color-making bacteria sounds difficult, I know, so here's how the science behind it works. Let's start with sound. As sound moves through a certain medium, whether that be a solid, liquid, or gas, it creates patterns. Sound travels as a wave, like one of those squiggly lines you doodle on your notes. On solids, these waves become visible when a powder is sprinkled over them. The visible pattern this powder creates is known as Chladni figures.

CHLADNI FIGURES

Chladni figures are named after Ernst Chladni, a German scientist from the 18th century. He studied different types of vibrations. One of his experiments involved taking a metal plate sprinkled with sand or salt, and brushing it with a bow, like the one used to play a violin, its side.[124] This produced a vibration that caused the sand or salt particles to move around on the plate, showing the way in which the sound traveled through the plate.

A similar phenomenon occurs in liquid mediums. In 1831, physicist Michael Faraday discovered that when sound travels through a liquid, the vibration created causes the water to ripple in the direction of the sound wave.[125]

These findings eventually lead to Cymatics, the study of waves and vibration. Luchtman and Siebenhaar started

---

124 Brian Malow, "Chladni Figures: Amazing Resonance Experiment," *Scientific American*, June 13, 2013.

125 *Vibrational Sounds Association*, "Faraday Waves Lesson," April 12, 2019, video, 3:09.

experimenting with how large particles like turmeric, a heavily pigmented yellow spice, could dye a textile in liquid when exposed to sound.[126] This approach was eventually applied on the bacterial level.

SOUND AND BACTERIA

So, what does sound have to do with bacteria anyway? Well, research shows that sound promotes the growth of bacteria. According to a paper published in *PeerJ* titled "Effects of sound exposure on the growth and intracellular macromolecular synthesis of *E. Coli* k-12," *E. Coli* k-12 exposed to sound waves had a greater biomass compared to those bacteria that were not exposed to sound waves.[127]

With all this information, Luchtman and Siebenhaar designed an experiment to see if they could use sound to manipulate the ways in which pigmenting bacteria produce color. They work with three different species of bacteria: *Janthinobacterium lividium*, *Arthrobacter agilis*, and *Micrococcus luteus*, which they refer to as their "heroes."[126] We should consider them our heroes as well—they could possibly save the textile dyeing industry.

J. lividium and *A. agilis* are found in soil. *M. luteus* is found not only in soil, but also on our skin, in water, and in dust.[126]

---

126 Laura Luchtman and Ilfa Siebenhaar, "Living Colour," Biodesign Research Project.

127 Shaobin Gu, Yongzhu Zhang, and Ying Wu, "Effects of sound exposure on the growth and intracellular macromolecular synthesis of *E. Coli* k-12," *PeerJ*, no. 4 (2016).

J. *lividium* produces a purple pigment called violacein. Vienna Textile Lab works with *J. lividium* as well and produces a pigment with antimicrobial properties.[126] Antimicrobial properties allow bacteria to kill other microbes such as viruses, fungi, and other bacteria. Violacein has also been found to help battle leukemia.

A. agilis produces a pinkish-red pigment, known as carotenoid. Carotenoids are found in plants, algae, and bacteria that undergo photosynthesis.[128] Carotenoids help the organism absorb light during photosynthesis and give the organism its color.[128] Another interesting quality of carotenoids is that they are beneficial to humans because they act as antioxidants and have been found to protect us from eye disease.[128]

A. agilis' abilities are not limited to just enhancing our health. This species of bacteria also detoxifies a harmful chemical, hexavalent chromium, which is found in traditional textiles by reducing chromium (VI) to chromium (III).[129] When an element is reduced, it means that it gains electrons, or the tiny negatively charged particles.

M. luteus produces a yellow pigment, which is also a carotenoid. An interesting ability this bacterium possesses is that they absorb UV radiation. Imagine the how this will transform the clothing we wear.

---

128 Elizabeth J Johnson, "The role of carotenoids in human health," *Nutritional Clinical Care* 5, no. 2 (2002): 56-65.

129 M Megharaj, S Avudainayagam, and R Naidu, "Toxicity of hexavalent chromium and its reduction by bacteria isolated from soil contaminated with tannery waste," *Curr Microbiol* 47, no. 1 (2003): 51-54.

Another important quality about these three species of bacteria is that they are non-pathogenic. Non-pathogenic bacteria are bacteria that will not cause infections in humans. They are just your friendly, neighborhood bacteria.

When bacteria produce pigment on textile without the influence of sound, they create a tie-dye pattern on the fabric.

EXPERIMENTING WITH BACTERIA AND SOUND

Luchtman and Siebenhaar created an audio system. With the help of Sound Engineer Eduard von Dommelen, they created an audio system with four different speakers to provide a range of frequencies.[130] Next to the sound system, they placed a petri dish with a liquid medium containing the bacteria and the textile to be dyed.[130] The bacteria dye the textiles live. Through their experimentation, they found that the bacteria that were exposed to sound-dyed textiles held a more uniform and evenly dyed finish.[130] It takes three days for the bacteria to dye a textile an even, completely solid color.

Bacteria like to grow where there is food and oxygen. The addition of sound creates a resonance that causes the food and oxygen to spread evenly throughout the liquid medium, allowing the bacteria to produce an even dye on the textile.

Amongst the three superhero bacteria, there was one that was better suited for dyeing textiles. *J. lividium* produced the best dyeing results and was the easiest to work with.[130] *M. luteus*

---

130 Laura Luchtman and Ilfa Siebenhaar, "Living Colour," Biodesign Research Project.

was the most challenging to work with because the pigment would not attach to the fabric.[130] A possible explanation for this discrepancy could be the chemical structure of each pigment.

When a dark pink fabric dyed from *A. agilis* is exposed to light, it fades away. While this may seem like a disadvantage, Luchtman and Siebenhaar see it as a fashion-forward opportunity. "We can take your favorite t-shirt, dye it in [a] seasonal color, darker more saturated shades in winter that gradually fade to lighter shades in spring, and by the end of summer, we can dye your t-shirt all over again in a new trendy color."[131]

Along with the pigments that do not easily adhere to the fabric, other challenges come with working with bacteria as well. Each species of bacteria requires a specific temperature and environment for optimal growth. Additionally, as little as they may be, bacteria are living organisms, so they have their own agency. They do what they want to do, not necessarily what you want them to do.

The bacteria of Living Colour showed their dyeing potential in a collaboration with Puma titled "Design to Fade."[132] The pieces in this project included windbreakers, muscle tees, and sneakers, which were all dyed with a light purple tie-dye pattern. This project illustrates how bacteria do have a place in the textile dyeing industry. All the pieces in this collaboration resembled the type of trendy athletic-wear you'd find in any department store.

---

131 *Tedx Talks,* "Rethinking the way clothes are colored | Laura Luchtman & Ilfa Siebenhaar | TEDxRotterdam," April 17, 2019, video, 12:#2.

132 "Design to Fade," Puma, accessed October 8, 2020.

Collaborating with scientists, Luchtman and Siebenhaar developed a research project that could eventually change the way we approach textile dyeing. "We don't have a scientific background at all. We are designers and it's really great that they can research our questions."[133] When designers collaborate with scientists, this creates an unstoppable team that has the ability to solve many questions surrounding sustainability and the fashion industry. This shouldn't seem strange, considering much of the dyeing process requires a basic background in chemistry.

"We, as a new generation of designers, can grow and tweak our materials and use this in a positive way."[133] If designers change the way they look at, choose, and even create materials, then maybe we can start bringing attention to the way we think about what goes into what we wear.

The current textile dyeing process uses toxic dyes that are harmful for us and our environment. Pigmenting bacteria produce dyes consisting of antioxidants and antimicrobials, which are beneficial for our health. Bacterial dyes are biodegradable. When we wear clothes, our skin comes in direct contact with whatever was put into making them.

Bacteria have already proven their textile dyeing ability. When it comes to changing the way we color our clothing, the solution is simple—dye with bacteria and create living colors.

---

133 *Kukka,* "The Future of Living Materials," October 10, 2018, video, 02:47.

CHAPTER 15

FINDING YOUR FAVORITE HUUE OF DENIM

Blue jeans are a staple item in any wardrobe. They go with everything and can be worn for every occasion. Have you ever wondered what gives this iconic piece its signature blue color? The process of getting that perfect shade of blue isn't as pretty as the final product. In fact, the way we are currently processing indigo dye is environmentally damaging. Indigo dye processing produces waste that ultimately pollutes our freshwater resources. Huue is one company that hopes to change the ways we create indigo dye by replacing indigo dying factories with bacteria.

THE ENVIRONMENTAL IMPACT

The indigo that dyes our jeans is chemically synthesized from petroleum, formaldehyde, and hydrogen cyanide. Not only is indigo derived from chemicals, it also is not soluble in water. As a result, the process of using indigo as a dye requires additional chemical reducing agents. These reducing agents pollute the environment, specifically bodies of water.

Breaking down the ingredients at the chemical level, in a process known as the Pfleger method, the synthesis of indigo begins with crude oil.[134] The oil undergoes several reactions to become benzene, which is converted into aniline.[134] Formaldehyde, hydrogen cyanide, and sodium hydroxide react with aniline to form a compound known as N-Phenylglycine.[1] In order to form Indigo, N-Phenylglycine must react with potassium hydroxide, sodium hydroxide, and sodamide.[134]

I don't know how you feel about all of these chemicals, but as someone who took organic chemistry in college, they sound pretty scary to me. Not only do these molecules have scary names, they also have scary effects like polluting rivers that people use as a source for drinking and bathing.

In 2016, *The Washington Post* published an article on the effects of the indigo dye plant on workers. Vijayakumar Varathan worked in indigo dye plants in India for fifteen years. In his early thirties, he developed a skin condition that caused his skin to peel off.[135] This is only one anecdotal account of a worker. What other side effects have workers experienced? No one has studied the long-term effects of working in indigo dyeing plants, or what happens when people use water polluted by dye plants.

---

134 Nicholas Wenner and Matther Forkin, "Indigo: Sources, process and possibilities," *Fibershed,* June 2017.

135 Esha Chhabra, "The dirty secret about your clothes," *The Washington Post,* December 30, 2016.

According to The Borgen Project, in Mumbai, India, the water of the Mithi River became so polluted with indigo dye that the fur of stray dogs began turning blue when they went for a swim.[136] If there is enough byproduct in the river to dye the fur of stray dogs, it probably has many other effects as well that we aren't aware—we do not have long term studies on the side effects of using this polluted water.

A NEW HUUE FOR DENIM

Huue, a California based company, found a new method to making your jeans green—not literally, but rather giving your jeans their iconic blue color without all the nasty chemicals and toxic byproducts.

Before Huue became a company, it started out as a project for a bioengineering competition at Berkley called iGEM, which was initiated by John Dueber's lab. Tammy Hsu, who is the current Chief Scientific Officer at the company, joined the lab when it started to work on this project. It became her thesis while she was completing her PhD at Berkeley for the last six years. In 2019, when she was getting ready to graduate, she decided to commercialize her findings and Huue was born.

Michelle Zhu, CEO of Huue, describes the excitement of transitioning a scientific advancement to a company, "It's a lot of fun to build a company around a core scientific advancement. A lot of years of work have gone into developing the product side of this before it actually came to be a company."

---

136 Kayla Cammarota, "Indigo Dye is Affecting the Water Supply in India," *The Borgen Project*, April 12, 2019.

THE INDIGO DYEING INDUSTRY'S CURRENT PROBLEMS

The industry's current method of creating dye presents two problems: dye is derived from petroleum and other carcinogenic chemicals and indigo is water insoluble, requiring additional toxic chemicals for its application.

Zhu explains how Huue was able to tackle both of these challenges. "We solved the first part of the problem by using fermentation technology, so you can feed sugar to programmed bacteria, and they will secrete an indigo precursor instead of relying on petroleum." This indigo precursor is a molecule that precedes indigo in the chemical process.

"When you combine the precursor with a separate enzyme, you are actually able to create a direct liquid indigo solution. This is applicable for dyeing and will help to eliminate some of the additional chemicals that are used in the dye application process." With this process, indigo is ready to be used as a dye for denim without those additional toxic chemicals, eliminating the waste that ends up in precious water resources.

E. COLI: THE NEW INDIGO DYE FACTORY

So how does Huue develop their dye? As Zhu explained, Huue is using bacteria and fermentation to create their indigo dye. Specifically, they use bacteria *E. coli* as a means of producing dye. "*E. coli* are one of the most fundamental, simple to work with organisms in terms of bioengineering. It keeps things relatively simple in terms of the programming and literature. For industrial products, *E. coli* is a very helpful organism for mass production and industrialization."

It's easy to associate *E. coli* with the negative effects it creates when ingested, which may cause some apprehension around the idea of using it as a means of production. Zhu dispels these concerns. She explains that no bacteria will end up on the jeans. *E. coli* is simply used as a vehicle to produce the dye. She says, "Sometimes when people hear *E. coli*, I think they definitely get a little bit nervous." The bacteria are like the factory, and the dye is the resulting product. No bacteria end up on the final product, they are just the means of production.

CREATING INDIGO DYE IN *E. COLI*

The biochemical process Huee employs is meticulously explained in a journal article titled "Employing a biochemical protecting group for a sustainable indigo dyeing strategy." The article explains that the method simulates the natural biochemical pathway found in the Japanese indigo plant *P. tinctorium*.[4] In the leaves of this plant, an organic compound known as indole reacts with oxygen to produce indoxyl, which is the molecule that precedes indigo.[4] Indoxyl has the chemical formula C_8H_7NO. The molecule is a benzene ring (a hexagon with three alternating lines on the inside) bound to a heterocyclic amine with four carbons and a hydroxyl group (an oxygen bound to a carbon).

A heterocyclic molecule refers to a molecule that is cyclic, so all the atoms are connected in the structure. An amine refers to a nitrogen atom that is bound to three different atoms. The importance of understanding the structure of this little molecule is what allows us to manipulate it. This different group with difficult sounding names has distinct properties that determine their reactivity, and whether the molecule reacts or not determines what will be made. In the indoxyl molecule, the hydroxyl group is considered to be reactive. If the group is oxidized, which mean the oxygen loses the hydrogen and forms a double bond with the carbon its attached to, then this would form indigo.[137] Oxidation does not occur at this step, rather the hydroxyl group is glycosylated, or a glucose group replaces the hydrogen molecule to which the oxygen molecule was initially bound.[138] The importance of this step is that it creates a protecting group around the oxygen.[138]

Protecting groups prevent a reactive molecule from reacting to the first compound that enables its reactive tendencies and allows for a more directed reaction. This gives the chemist the natural pathway to choose the compound with which the highly reactive molecule reacts with most. All it requires is removing the protecting group and presenting the desired compound to the reactive molecule. The glycosylated indoxyl molecule is called indican, which, unlike indigo, is colorless.[138]

So, what activates the indigo color in the leaves of *P. tinctorium?* Apparently, the indigo color is activated when the tissue in the leaves is damaged.[138] Plant cells hold a structure known as a vacuole, which is like a storage space. In *P. tinctorium,* the vacuole is where indican is stored.[138] The chloroplasts of a plant cell are structures that contain chlorophyll, which gives plants their green color.

---

137 Tammy M Hsu et al., "Employing a biochemical protecting group for sustainable indigo dyeing strategy," *Nat Chem Biol* 14, (2018):256-261.

138 Ibid.

In *P. tinctorium,* the chloroplasts contain an enzyme known as β-glucosidase. An enzyme is a biological catalyst, an agent that speeds up the rate of reactions in nature. When these two structures, the vacuole and chloroplasts, are damaged in the leaves of *P. tinctorium,* indican and β-glucosidase mix.[138] The mixing of these two causes β-glucosidase to break down indican to indoxyl.[138] Indoxyl, with its highly reactive hydroxyl group, then oxidizes to create indigo via an intermediate called leucoindigo. An intermediate is a molecule that precedes the desired product.[139]

Huue recreated this natural process using *E. coli* as the vehicle for production. Isolating the gene from *P. tinctorium* that enables this process and inserting it into *E. coli* gives *E. coli* the ability to biosynthesize indoxyl and create the protected compound indican. When you want to use the indigo as a dye, all you need to do is cleave the indican with β-glucosidase, and your indigo is ready to go.

In comparison to the industry's current process, Huue eliminates the need of harsh chemicals to create indigo and the harsh chemicals required to apply it.

THE FUTURE

I don't know about you, but I see more jeans in our future OOTDs. This discovery may create the potential of all our clothes to be dyed via bacteria biosynthesis. "We think that biotechnology and bioengineering have huge promise and opportunity in the future of color because all dyes today

---

139 "Indoxyl," National Library of Medicine, accessed March 19, 2020.

are chemically synthesized, meaning that we have a broader opportunity to do it via biosynthesis instead," Zhu says. While we have great potential here for dyeing a rainbow through this mechanism, Huue's current focus is on blue jeans. "For now, our focus is certainly indigo. We want to do that, and do it right to begin with, but we do have the vision of expanding to additional colors in the back of our minds. We'll continue research and work in the background in the coming year. Using the same principles, you create the same kind of sustainability."

These discoveries are incredible and create the possibility of a more sustainable textile dyeing industry. These discoveries are just being made, and there still may be some time before they are introduced into the fashion industry at the production level. "I'm hopeful that within the next few years we're able to get something out there, and, at least in full scale, be able to start to pilot some products. These solutions take time and research, so it may take years before we see this type of biotechnology in the mainstream fashion industry. We are working towards commercialization right now, but I will say, broadly, that would be a really fast timeline for most people in the industry. Generally, these types of solutions take many years and millions and millions of dollars," Zhu says.

While these developments will take time to affect our fast fashion world, they present us fashion enthusiasts with a more sustainable reality for how our favorite pair of jeans are made. Zhu says, "My hope would be with the introduction of our product that we very much shape the narrative of what can help contribute to a pair of cleaner jeans, and [Huue is] kind of like a label or seal to represent sustainability on a pair of jeans."

Companies like Huue are just the beginning of creating a more sustainable fashion industry. Bacteria are very small organisms, but they have the potential to disrupt the future of textile dyeing by creating more sustainable practices and a greener pair of jeans.

PART 5

CONCLUSION

CONCLUSION

So, what is in store for the future of fashion? With biotechnology emerging as a blossoming field on the frontier of almost every field, it is not surprising that it will slowly be taking over the fashion industry, as well. This is not just an expectation, but also a necessity. Fast Fashion, fueled by influencer culture and consumerism, disregards its ethical and environmental impacts. It focuses on satisfying the consumer's insatiable desire to become Instagram famous and fill the pockets of the major companies that profit from this desire. The fashion industry cannot continue to go on like this.

We must change our attitudes towards our clothes, environment, and our relationship with them. Biogarmentry is one project that brings attention to the concept of developing a relationship with our clothes. Psychologically, we have a tendency to treat living things with better care. Maybe if we change our means of production to biological systems, we will develop a greater responsibility toward the materials that go into making the fabric as well as the way we treat the fabric itself.

Using microbes to produce material for fabric is one solution that can reduce the negative effect the fashion industry has on the environment. Lee explains that microbes are efficient. She says, "What excites me about using microbes is their efficiency. So, we only grow what we need. There's no waste."[140] The process that goes into creating material from microbes is waste-free.

Let's say you want a new jacket. You could biodegrade your old one, and then you could make your new one from the sugar waste of a food processing plant. Nature looks to recycle and recreate. Microbes take waste and transform it into a source of energy for themselves. The jacket you no longer want is now a source of food for the microorganisms and bacteria in the earth. Reuse and recycling have the potential to transform the fashion industry's current means of apparel production.

We can go back to traditional methods of creating textiles, ones which came before the Industrial Revolution. Theanne Schiros, Co-founder of Algiknit, found a solution for creating material grown from microbes into textiles using the ancient Native American technique of tanning and smoking hides. She says, "Indigenous processes, like those of nature itself, have been practiced and perfected over millennia."[141]

Material grown from microbes does not translate well into textiles. The resulting material does not have strength,

---

140 Suzanne Lee, "Grow Your Own Clothes," filmed February 2011 at TED2011 in Longbeach, CA, video, 06:25.

141 *TED,* "BioDesign: The (R)evolution of Sustainable Fashion | Theanne Schiros | TEDxFIT," January 4, 2018, video, 17:55.

durability, nor is it water resistant.[142] Schiros looked to the Native American processes of tanning and smoking, which produced soft hides that were pliable even after being exposed to water.[142] Using these techniques on the microbial material, Schiros was able to create a material that was three times stronger, three times more flexible, water proof, and flame retardant.[142]

The materials used to create textiles today typically have flame retardants that are associated with causing birth defects, cancer, reproductive issues, and autoimmune disorders.[142] This ancient technique is a natural way to make material flame-resistant without the harmful chemicals. Not only did this material become flame-retardant, it also had another interesting ability when kept in flames. Schiros exposed the material to flame with a 2000-degree torch until it became ash, and set it aside.[142] After an hour, the material returned back to its original state. Schiros says, "In my years as a material scientist, we've never seen anything like this."[2] The development of this type of material could be used to create uniforms for firefighters and open so many possibilities for creating more durable, sustainable fabrics.

The future of a sustainable fashion industry requires going back to nature and connecting with it on a deeper level. Maybe we won't finger-weave our textiles like the Native Americans once did, but we will use past techniques to perfect the research with the biotechnological tools we have already discovered.

---

142 *TED,* "BioDesign: The (R)evolution of Sustainable Fashion | Theanne Schiros | TEDxFIT," January 4, 2018, video, 17:55.

Biofabrication is already taking fashion to the next level, and it will help transform it into a more sustainable industry. We just need to take the blueprint nature has already laid out for us and use it to create a more sustainable means of production.

APPENDIX

___

INTRODUCTION

Lee, Suzanne. "Grow your own clothes." Filmed February 2011 at TED2011 in Long Beach, CA. Video, 06:25. https://ww.ted.com/talks/suzanne_lee_grow_your_own_clothes/transcript.

PART 1

CHAPTER 1

Arneson, Kyrstin. "Fashion Nova Already Knocked Off Looks From Kylie Jenner's Birthday Party." *Glamour,* August 11, 2018. https://ww.glamour.com/story/fashion-nova-kylie-jen-ner-birthday-outfits.

Bailey, Alyssa. "Exclusive: How Kylie Jenner Helped Create Her $8,000 Custom LaBourjoisie Jumpsuit For Her 21st Birthday," *Elle,* August 10, 2018. https://www.elle.com/fashion/celebrity-style/a22697731/kylie-jenner-labourjoisie-jumpsuit-21st-birthday-jumpsuit-details-sketches/.

Castiel, Daniella. "How Fashion Affects People and the Environment." *Sierra Club,* Novemebr 29, 2016. https://www.sierraclub.org/planet/2016/11/how-fashion-affects-people-and-environment.

Eriksen, Marcus, Laurent C. M. Lebreton, Henry S. Carson, Martin Thiel, Charles J. Moore, Jose C. Borerro, Francois Galgani, Peter G. Ryan, and Julia Reisser, "Plastic Pollutionin the World's Oceans: More than 5 Trillion Plastic Pieces Weighing ovr 250,000 Tons Afloat at Sea." *PLoS ONE* 9, no. 12 (2014): e111913. https://doi.org/10.1371/journal.pone.0111913.

Fashion Nova. "Birthday Bash Sequin Romper." Accessed May 4, 2020. https://ww.fashionnova.com/collections/kylie/products/birthday-bash-sequin-romper-pink.

Hutton, Guy. "Cleanng Up One of the World's Most Pollute Places." *World Bank Blogs,* December 19, 2013. https://blogs.worldbank.org/water/cleaning-one-world-s-most-polluted-places.

"Indonesia's Most Polluted River." *Al Jazeera,* May 3, 2018. https://www.aljazeera.com/program/101-east/2018/5/3/indonesias-most-polluted-river/

Kosuth, Mary, Sherri A. Mason, and Elizabeth V. Wattenberg. "Anthropogenc contamination of tap water, beer, and sea salt." *PLoS ONE* 13, no. 4 (2018): e0194970. https://doi.org/10.1371/journal.pone.0194970.

Moulds, Josephine. "Child labour in the fashion supply chain." *The Guardian.* n. d. https://labs.theguardian.com/unicef-child-labour/.

Napper, Imogen E, Richard C. Thimpson. "Release of synthetic microplastic plastic fibers from domestic washing machines: Effects of fabric type and washing conditions." *Marine Pollution Bulletin* 112, no. 1-5 (2016): 39-45.https://doi.org/10.1016/j.marpolbul.2016.09.025.

National Institutes of Health. "Microplastics." Accessed May 4, 2020. https://toxtown.nlm.nih.gov/sources-of-exposure/microplastics.

Panno, Samuel V. Walton R. Kelly, John Scott, Wei Zhang, Rachel E. McNeish, Nancy Holm, Timothy J. Hoellein, and Elizabeth L. Baranski. "Microplastic Contamination in Karst Goundwaer Systems." *Groundwater* 57, no. 2 (2019): 189-196. https:///doi.org/10.1111/gwat.12862.

Paździor, Katarzyna, Julita Wrębiak, Anna Kelpacz-Smólka, Marta Gmurek, Lucyna Bilińska, Lech Kos, Jadwiga Sójka-Ledakowicz. "Influence of ozonation and biodegradation on toxicity of industrial textile wastewater." *Journal of Environmental Management* 195, no. 2 (2017): 166-173. https://doi.org/10.1016/j.jenvman.2016.06.055.

Pulse of the Fashion Industry (Global Fashion Agenda and The Boston Cosulting Group, 2017). 11. Accessed May 4, 2020. https://stattic1.squarespace.com/static/5810348d59cc68e52b7d-9ba/t/596454f715db35061ea63e/1499747644232/Pulse-of-the-Fashion-Industry_2017.pdf.

Remy, Nathalie, Eveline Speelman, and Steven Swartz. "Style that's sustainable: A new fast fashion formula." *McKinsey & Company,* October 20, 2016. https://www.mckinsey.com/busi-

ness-functions/sustainability/our-insights/style-that's-sustain-
able-a-new-fast fashion-formula.

Resnick, Brian. "More than ever, out clothes are made of pastic.
Just washing them can pollute the oceans." *Vox.* Janruary 11,
2019. https://www.vox.com/the-goods/2018/9/19/17800654/
clothes-plastic-pollution-polyester-washing-machine.

Theuws, Martje and Puline Overeem. "Flawed Fabrics: The abuse of
girls and women workers in the South Asian Textile Industry
(Centre for Research on Multinational Corporations and India
Committee of the Netherlands)." 39. Accessed May 4, 2020.
https://www.indianet.nl/pdf/FlawedFabrics.pdf.

Vatvani, Chandni. "The toxic waste that enters Indonesia's Ciatrum River, one of the World's Most Polluted." *Channel News
Asia,* April 14, 2018. https://www.channelnewsasia.com/news/
asia/indonesia-ciatrum-river-worlds-most-polluted-tox-
ic-waste-10124436.

Wieczorek, Alina M., Liam Morrison, Petter L. Croot, A. Loiose
Allcock, Eoin MacLoughlin, Olivier Savard, Hannah Brownlow,
and Thomas K. Doyle. "Frequency of Microplastics in Mesopelagic Fishes from the Northwest Atlantic." *Frontiers in Marine
Science* 5, (2018): 39. https://doi.org/10.3389/fmars.2018.00039.

Zubcevic, Irena, Simone Cipriani, Maria Beatriz Mello da Cunha,
Michael Stanley-Jones, Karen Newman, Lillian Liu, and Niclas
Sevenningsen. "Fashion and the SDGs: what role for the UN?"
Program for the International Conference Center Geneva,
Geneva, Switzerland, March 2018. https://www.unece.org/fil-

eadmin/DAM?RCM_Website?RFSD_2018_Side_event_sustainable_fashion.pdf.

CHAPTER 2

Carocci, Max. "Clad with the 'Hir of Trees': A History of Native American Spanish Moss Textile Industries." *Textile History* 41, no. 1 (2013): 3-27. https://doi.org/10.1179/174329510x12 670196126485.

Council of Fashion Designers of America. "Rayon (Viscose)." Accessed August 24, 2020.

CrashCourse, "Coal, Steam, and the Industrial Revolution: Crash Course World History #32," August 30, 2012. Video, 11:05. https://www.youtube.com/watch?v=zhL5DCizj5c&vl=en.

History Crunch (blog). "Working Conditions during the Industrial Revolution." Las modified July 29, 2019. https://ww.history-crunch.com/working-conditions-in-the-industrial-revolution. html#/.

"How is leather tanned?." Accessed Decemebr 30, 2019. https://bestleather.org/leather-tanning/.

Kirwan, Padraig. "The Emergent Land: Nature and Ecology in Native American Expressive Forms." English Department University of California Davis, 1999. https://www.udc.ie/pages/99/articles/kirwan.pdf.

Lee, Suzanne. "Why Biofabrication is the Next Industrial Revolution." Filmed July 2019 at TEDSummit, Edinburg, Scotland.

Video, 12:12. https://www.ted.com/talks/suzanne_lee_why_
biofabrication_is_the_next_industrial_revolution/trn-
script#t-2058.

Moulds, Josephine. "Child labour in the fashion supply chain."
The Guardian. n.d. https://labs.theguardian.com/unicef-child-
labour/.

Suzanne Dalton (blog). "Nativs American Art: Native American
Finger Weaving In the Eastern Forests." Accessed December 30,
2019. https://suzannedalton.com/crossvillagerugworks/www/
Native_Amer_Tech_Atr.pdf.

The Patriot Act. "The Ugly Truth of Fast Fashion | The Patriot
Act." November 25, 219. Video, 29:02. https://www.youtube.
com/watch?v=xGF3ObOBbac&t=4s.

"Traditional Buckskin." *Biskink.* December 2012. https://www.
choctawnation.com/sites/default/files/2015/09/29/Biski-
nik2012_12_original.pdf.

CHAPTER 3

Biofabricate. "Biofabricate is a platform for biomaterial innovators
and consumer brands growing a sustainable future." Accessed
May 11, 2020. https://www.biofabricate.co/about.

Chu, Jennifer. "Researhcers Design Moisture-Responisve Workot
Suit." *MIT News,* May 19, 2017. https://news.mit.edu/2017/mois-
ture-responsive-workout-suit-0519.

Cleveland Clinic Health Essentials. "The Best Way You Can Get More Collagen." May 15, 2018. Accessed May 11, 2020. https://health.clevelandclinic.org/the-best-way-you-can-get-more-collagen/.

Fritz, Monika, Angela M. Belcher, Manfred Radmacher, Deron A. Walters, Paul K. Hansma, Galen D. Stucky, Daniel E. Morse, and Stephen Mann. "Flat Pearls from Biofabrication of Organized Composites on Inorganic Substrates." *Nature* 371, no. 6495 (1994): 49-51. https://doi.org/10.1038/371049a0.

Grol Jürgen, Thomas Boland, Torsten Blunk, Jason A Burdick, Dong-Woo Cho, Paul D Dalton, Brian Derby et al. "Biofabrication: reappraising the definition of an evolving field." *Biofabrication* 8, no. 1 (2016). https://doi.org/10.10.1088/1758-5090/8/1/013001.

Lee, Andrew, Andrew Hudson, Daniel Shiwarski, J.W. Tashman, Thomas Hinton, Sai Yerneni, Jacqueline Biley, Phil Campbell, and Adam W Feinberg. "3d Bioprinting of collagen to rebuild componenets of the human heart." *Science* 365. No. 6452 (2019): 482-487. https://doi.org/10.1126.science.aav9051.

Liu, Yi, Eunkyung Kim, Reza Ghodssi, Gary W Rubloff, James N Culver, William E Bentley, and Gregory F Payne. "Biofabrication to build the biology-device interface." *Biofabrication* 2, no. 2 (2010). https://doi.org/10.1088/1758-5082/2/2/022002.

Luo, Xiaolong. "Biofabrication in Microfluidics: A Converging Fabrication Paradigm to Exploit Biology in Microsystems." *Journal of Bioengineering and Biomedical Science* 2, no. 2 (2012). https://doi.org/10.4172/2155-9538.1000e104.

The Business Fashion. "Welcome to the Era of Biofabrication | Andras Forgacs | #BoFVOICES 2017." April 23, 2018. Video, 23:51. https://www.youtube.com/watch?vJs1A9oh-JAw.

PART 2

The Buisness of Fashion. "Welcome to the Era of Biofabrication | Andras Forgacs | #BoFVOICES 2017." April 23, 2018. Video, 23:51. https://www.youtube.com/watch?v=Js1A9oh-JAw.

CHAPTER 4

Business of Fashion. "Andras Forgacs." Accessed May 9, 2020. https://www.businessoffashion.com/community/people/andras-forgacs.

Chen, Kuo-Wen, Lung-Chieh Lin, and Wen-Shing Lee "Analyzing the Carbon Footprint of Finished Bovine Leather: A Case Study of Aniline Leather." *Energy Procedia* 61, (2014): 1063-1066. https://doi.org/10.1016/j.egypro.2014.11.1023.

Food and Agriculture Organization of the United Nations. "Key Facts and Findings." Accessed May 9, 2020. https://www.fao.org/news/story/en/item/197623/icode/.

Forgacs, Andras. "Leather and Meat without killing animals." Filmed June 2013 at TedGlobal 2013, Edinburg, Scotland. Video, 8:35. https://www.ted.com/talks/andras_forgacs_leather_and_meat_without_killing_animals/transcript#t-556631.

Kesar, Gayatri. "Material Story: Zoa." *Material Connexion,* January 9, 2018. https://www.materialconnexion.com/material-story-zoa/.

Modern Meadow. "FAQ." Accessed May 9, 2020. http://www.modernmeadow.com/faq (site discontinued).

Siegle, Lucy. "Is it Time to Give Up Leather?" *The Guardian,* March 13, 2016. https://www.theguardian.com/fashion/2016/mar/13/is-it-time-to-give-up-leather-animal-welfare-ethical-lucy-siegle.

Shoulders, Matthew D. and Ronald T. Raines. "Collagen Structure and Stability." *Annual Review of Biochemistry,* 78 (2009): 929-958. https://www.doi.org/10.1146/annure.biochem.77.032207.120833.

"Taiwan outproduces East Asia in Carbon Emissions." *Taipei Times,* October 14, 2011. http://www.taipeitimes.com/News/taiwan/archives/2011/10/14/2003515719.

CHAPTER 5

Bolt Threads. "Bolt Technology-Meet Microsilk™." Accessed May 24, 2020. https://boltthreads.com/technology/microsilk.

Bolt Threads. "Bolt Technology-Meet Mylo™." Accessed May 24, 2020. https://boltthreads.com/technology/mylo.

Feldman, Amy. "Clothes From A Petri Dish: $700 Million Bolt Threads May Have Cracked the Code On Spider Silk." *Forbes.* August 15, 2018. https://www.forbes.com/sites/

amyfeldman/2018/08/14/clothes-from-a-petri-dish-700-million-bolt-threads-may-have-cracked-the-code-on-spider-silk/#62a7ca24bda1.

Gilbride, Kristen. "You're Wearing Plastic: The Synthetic Plastic Takeover." Global Fashion Exchange (blog). April 16, 2019. https://www.gobalfashionxchange.org/gfxmag/2019/4/16/synthetic-fabric-takeover.

Kickstarter. "This 'leather' bag is animal-free and not petroleum based!" Accessed May 24, 2020. https://www.kickstarter.com/projects/boltprojects/the-mylo-driver-bag.

Purves, William K. "Why is spider silk so strong?" *Scientific America*. October 16, 2006. https://www.scientificamerican.com/article/why-is-spider-silk-so-str/.

Romer, Lin, Thomas Scheiber. "The elaborate structure of spider silk: structure and function of a natural high performance fiber." *Prion* 2, no. 4 (2008): 154-161. https://www.doi.org/10.4161/pri.2.4.7490.

Soth, Amelia. "The Tangled History of Weaving with Spider Silk." *JSTOR Daily*. November 15, 2018. https://daily.jstor.org/the-tangled-history-of-weaving-with-spider-silk.

van Beek, J. D, S. Hess, F. Vollrath, B. H. Meier. "The molecular structure of spider dragline silk" Folding and orientation of the protein backbone." *Proceedings of the National Academy of Sciences of the United States of America* 99, no. 16, (2002): 10266-10271. https://doi.org/10.1073/pnas.152162299.

CHAPTER 6

Common Objective. "Fibre Briefing: Leather." February 1, 2018. Accessed September 13, 2020. https://www.commonobjective. co/article/fibre-briefing-leather.

Dorset Wildlife Trust. "Birch polypore." Accessed May 14, 2020. https://www.dorsetwildlifetrust.org.uk/wildlife-explorer/ fungi/birch-polypore.

Grover, Andrea. "The Future is Fungal: Interview with Phil Ross." *Glasstire,* September 8, 2012. https://glasstire.com/2012/09/08/ the-future-fungal-interview-with-phil-ross/.

PETA. "Leather: Animals Abused and Killed for their Skins." Accessed September 13, 2020. https://www.peta.org/issues/ animals-used-for-clothing/animals-used-clothing-factsheets/ leather-animals-abused-killed-skins/.

Reishi™. "Fabricating With Reishi™: Through the eyes of master rather artisan, Béatrice Amblard." Accessed May 14, 2020. https://www.madewithreishi.com/stories/fabricating-with-reishi.

SciFri. "The Fungi in Your Future." November 16, 2016. Video, 5:22. https://www.youtube.com/watch?v=jBXGFOk5_Rs.

The New School. "Mycotecture: architecture grown out of mushrooms | Parsons The New School for Design." April 11, 2014. Video, 1:15:42. https://www.youtube.com/watch?v=7q5i9p0Yc3w.

Woven Multimedia. "Sophia Wang of MycoWorks-Youtube."
September 9, 2016. Video, 18:27. https://www.youtube.com/
watch?v=U79K2dMF7dY.

CHAPTER 7

"How Much Do Our Wardrobes Cost the Environment?" The World
Bank. Accessed September 3, 2020. https://www.worldbank.
org/en/news/feature/2019/09/23/costo-moda-medio-ambiente.

CHAPTER 8

Isabel Fletcher (website). "Offcut One." Accessed June 3, 2020.
https://isabelfletcher.com/offcut-one.

Rastogi, Nina Shen. "The Eco-Perils of Cheap Décor." *Slate,* September 15, 2009. https://slate.com/technology/2009/09/is-fake-
wood-furniture-bad-for-the-environment.html.

PART 3

McFall-Johnsen, Morgan. "These Facts Show How Unsustainable
the Fashion Industry Is." *World Economic Forum,* January 21,
2020. https://www.weforum.org/agenda/2020/01/fashion-in-
dustry-carbon-unsustainable-environmental-pollution.

PETA. "Wool, Fur, and Leather: Hazardous to the Environment."
Accessed June 13, 2020. https://www.peta.org/issues/animals-
used-for-clothing/animals-used-clothing-factsheets/woool-
fur-leather-hazardous-environment.

CHAPTER 9

Design Indaba. "Aleksandra Gosiewski talks seaweed fashion and the next stage of biotech." April 19, 2020. Video, 6:53. https://www.youtube.com/watch?v=U8cAFaLWbpU&feature=emb_title.

FIT Newsroom. "AlgiKnit Wins a National Geographic Chasing Genius Award." Last modified September 18, 2017. https://news.fitnyc.edu/2017/09/18/algiknit-wins-a-national-geographic-chasing-genius-award/.

FIT Newsroom. "FIT Team Wins Biodesign Challenge." Last modified June 20, 2016. https://news.fitnyc.edu/2016/06/30/fit-team-wins-biodesign-challenge-at-moma/.

Friedman, Wendy. "In Conversation with Asta Skocir, Co-Founder of AlgiKnit" *Knitting Industry Creative,* February 22, 2018. https://www.knittingindustry.com/creative/interview-with-asta-skocir-co-founder-of-algiknit/.

Lee, Kuen Yong and David J Mooney. "Alginate properties and biomedical applications," *Progress in polymer science* 37, no. 1 (2012): 106-126. https://doi.org/10.1016/j.progpolymsci.2011.06.003.

TED. "BioDesign: The °evolution of Sustainable Fashion | Theanne Schiros | TEDxFIT." Janruary 4, 2018. Video, 17:55. https://www.youtube.com/watch?v=oaDmtThjH3U.

SynBioBeta. "AlgiKnit Closes $2.2M Seed Round to Develop Kelp-Derived Yarn." Last modified Novemebr 16, 2018. Htps://sunbiobeta.com/algiknit-closes-2-2m-seed-round-to-develop-kelp-derived-yarn/.

CHAPTER 10

Baldwin, S., M R Odio, S L Haines, R J O'Connor, J S Enlehart, and A T Lane. "Skin benefits from continuous topical administration of a zinc oxide/ petrolatum formulation by a novel disposable diaper." *Journal of the European Academy of Dermatology and Venereology* 15, no. 1 (2001): 5-11. https://doi.org/10.1046/j.0926-9959.2001.00002.x.

Kim, Ji Hye, Jae-Eun Lee, Kyoung Heon Kim, and Nam Too Kang. "Beneficial Effects of Marine Algae-Derived Carbohydrates for Skin Health." *Marine Drugs* 16, no. 11 (2018): 459. https://doi.org/10.3390/md16110459.

Pharm-Huy, Lien Ai, Hua He, and Chuong Pharm-Huy. "Free Radicals, Antioxidants in Disease and Health." *International Journal of Biomedical Science* 4, no. 2 (2008): 89-96. https://www.ncbi.nlm.nih.gov/pmc/articlrd/PMC3614697/.

Smartfiber AG (blog). "New confirmation to take care of antioxidantien on our skin with our SeaCell[TM] fiber." March 9, 2019. Accessed June 1, 2020. https://www. smartfiber.de/en/news/artikel/detail/News/new-confirmation-to-take-care-of-antioxidantien-on-our-skin-with-our-seacelltm-fiber/.

Smartfiber AG newsroom (blog). "SeaCell[TM]: The natural fiber with the skin-caring properties of pure seaweed." September 18,

2014. Accessed June 1, 2020. https://english.smartfibernews-room.de/index.php/news-wp/entry/seacell-the-natural-fiber-with-the-skin-caring-properties-of-pure-seaweed.

Wollina, Uwe, Nadine Schmidt, Diana Mühle, Gesina Hansel, "Clinical experiences with an antimicrobial bed equipment using zinc-smartcell™ fibers for pronounced atopic dermatitis." *Cosmetic Medicine* 4, no. 23 (2019): 20-23. https://www.smart-fiber.de/fileadmin/user_upload/Cosmetic_Medicine_0119.pdf.

Zheng, Shoakai, Chunxia Chen, Chao Duan, Huichao Hu, Hailong Li, Jianguo Li, Yishan Liu, Xiaojan Ma, Jaroslave Stavik, and Yonghao Ni. "Regenerated Cellulose by the Lyocell Process, a Brief eview of the Process and Properties." *BioResources* 13, no. 2 (2018): 4577-4592. https://bioresources.cnr.ncsu.edu/resources/regenerated-cellulose-by-the-lyocel-process-a-brief-review-of-the-process-and-properties/.

CHAPTER 11 PIÑATEX.

Philippine Folklife Museum Foundation. "History and Origin of Piña." Accessed June 11, 2020. https://philippinefolklifemu-seum.org/portfolio-items/history-and-origin-of-pina/.

Piñatex. "About us." Accessed June 11, 2020. https://www.anan-as-anam.com/about-us/.

Piñatex. "/#Made from Piñatex." Products. Accessed June 11, 2020. https://www.ananas-anam.com/products-2/.

Moulds, Josephine. "Child labour in the fashion supply chain." *The Guardian.* https://labs.theguardian.com/uncief-child-labour/.

My Barong. "History of the Barong Tagalog." Accssed June 11, 2020. http://mybarong2.com/history-barong-tagalog-art-99.html.

Ranson, Beth. "The True Cost of Colour: The impact of textile dyes on water systems." *Fashion Revolution.* https://www.fashion-revolution.org/the-true-cost-of-colour-the-impact-of-textile-dyes-on-water-systems/.

United States Department of Labor. "Hexavalent Chromium." Accessed June 11, 2020. https://www.osha.gov/SLTC/hexava-lentchromium/.

PART 4

Drew, Deborah and Genevieve Yehounme. "The Apparel Industry's Environmental Impact in 6 Graphics." *World Resources Institute* (blog), July 5, 2017. https://www.wri.org/blog/2017/07/apparel-industrys-environmental-impact-6-graphics.

Hossain, Laila, Sumit Kanti Sarker, and Mohidus Samad Khan. "Evalution of present and future wastewater impacts of textiles dyeing industries in Bangladesh." *Environmental Development* 26, (2018): 23-33. https://doi.org/10.1016/j.envdev.2018.03.005.

Standout Practices at High-Performing Bangladeshi Textile Mills: How Top Resource-Efficient Factories in Bangladesh Save Money and Curb Pollution (NRDC), 2. Accessed February 4, 2020. https://www.nrdc.org/sites/default/files/cbd-textile-mills-standout-practices-bangladesh.pdf.

CHAPTER 12

Bentley, S.D., K. F. Chater, A. –M. Cerdaeño-Tárraga, G. L. Challis, N. R. Thomson, K. D. James, D. E. Harris et al. "Complete genome sequence of the mdel actinomycete *Streptomyces Coelicolor* A3(2)." *Nature* 417, (2002): 141-147. https://doi.org/10.1038/417141a.

Chizea, Natsai Audrey. "Fashion has pollution problem-can we fix it?" Filmed Octover 2017 at TED@BCG Milan, Milan, Italy. Video, 12:45. https://www.ted.com/talks/natsai_audrey_chieza_fashion_has_apollution_problem_can_biology_fix_it/transcript.

Faber Futures. "Nature-Cooper Hewitt Design Triennial." October 5, 2019. https://faberfutures.com/nature-cooper-hewitt-design-triennial/.

Faber Futures. "On the Faber Futures x Ginkgo Residency." April 6, 2018. https://faberfutures.com/biology-is-now-a-design-space-space-and-biologists-design/.

Hassaan, Mohamed A. and Ahmed El Nemr. "Health and Environmental Impacts of Dyes: Mini Review." *American Journal of Environmental Science and Engineering* 1, No. 3 (2017): 64-67. https://www.doi.org/10.11648/j.ajese.20170103.11.

Phipps, Lauren. "Just dye it: how this apparel company is developing water-and chemical-free textile tinting." *GreenBiz,* February 26, 2019. https://www.greenbiz.com/article/just-dye-it-how-apparel-company-developing-water-and-chemical-free-textile-tinting.

The Business of Fashion. "Making With Life: Design Driven Biology | Natsai Audrey Chieza, Faber Futures | #BoFVOICES 2018." May 29, 2019. Video, 15:57. https://www.youtube.com/watch?v=-joq3EogFDwE&feature=emb_title.

The Index Project. "Project Coelicolor." Accessed June 11, 2020. https://theindexproject.org/award/winnersandfinalists/project-coelicolor-body.

The Index Project. "Project Coelicolor." September 5, 2019. Video, 03:33. https://vimeo.com/358044486.

CHAPTER 13

ClimateLaunchpad. "Vienna Textile Lab pitch-ClimateLaunchpad Grand Finale." November 15, 2017. Video, 5:08. https://www.youtubecom/watch?v=ny6AoOFtWRE.

Kant, Rita. "Textile dyeing industry an environment hazard." *Natural Science* 4, no. 1 (2012). https://www.doi.org/10.4236/ns.2012.41004.

Valdes, Natalia, Paola Soto, Luis Cottet, Paula Alarcon, Alex Gonzalez, Antonio Castillo, Gino Corsini, and Mario Tello. "Draft genome sequence of *Janthinobacterium lividium* strain MTR reveals its mechanism of capnophilic behavior." *Standard Genomic Science,* no. 10 (2015): 110. https://doi.org/10.1186/s40793-015-0104-z.

CHAPTER 14

Gu, Shaobin, Yongzhu Zhang, and Ying Wu. "Effects of sounds exposure on the growth and intracellular macromolecular synthesis of *E. coli* k-12." *PeerJ*, no. 4 (2016). https://www.doi.org/10.7717/peerj.1920.

Johnson, Elizabeth J. "The role of carotenoids in human health." *Nutritional Clinical Care* 5, no. 2 (2002): 56-65. https://www.doi.org/10.1046/j.1523-5408.2002.00004.x.

Kukka. "The Future of Living Materials." October 19, 2018. Video, 02:47. https://vimeo.com/294452499.

Luchtman, Laura and Ilfa Siebenhaar. "Living Colour." Biodesign Research Project. https://issuu.com/kukkadesign/docs/living_colour-ibook.

Malow, Brian. "Chladni Figures: Amazing Resonance Experiment." *Scientific America,* June 13, 2013. https://blogs.scientificamerican.com/blout-seriously/chladni-figures-amazing-resonance-experiment/.

Megharaj, M, S Avudainayagam and R Naidu. "Toxicity of hexavalent chromium and its reduction by bacteria isolated from soil contaminated with tannry waste." *Curr Microbiol* 47, no. 1 (2003): 51-54. https://www.doi.org/10.1007/s00284002-3889-0.

Puma, "Designed to Fade." Accessed October 8, 2020. https://designtofade.puma.com/project/living-colours.

Tedx Talks, "Rethinking the way clothes are colored | Laura Luchtman & Ilfa Siebenhaar | TEDxRotterdam." April 17, 2019. Video, 12:32. http://www.youtube.com/watch?v=DXB3YtMWp0Y.

Vibrational Sounds Association. "Faraday Waves Lesson." April 12, 2019. Video, 3:09. https://www.youtube.com/watch?v=6hY-B3_6H6Jc.

CHAPTER 15

Cammarota, Kayla. "Indigo Dye is Affecting the Water Supply in India." *The Borgen Project,* April 12, 2019. https://borgenproject.org/indigo-dye-is-affecting-the-water-supply-in-india/.

Chhabra, Esha. "The dirty secret about your clothes." *The Washington Post,* December 30, 2016. https://www.washingtonpost.com/business/the-dirty-secret-about-your-clothes/2016/12/30/715ed0e6-bb20-11e6-94ac-3d324840106c_story.html.

Hsu, Tammy M, Ditte H Welner, Zachary N Russ, Bernardo Cervantes, Ramya L Prathuri, Paul D Adams, and John E Dueber, "Employing a biochemical protecting group for a sustainable indigo dyeing strategy." *Nat Chem Biol* 14, (2018): 256-261. https://doi.org/10.1038/nchembio.2552.

National Library of Medicine. "Indoxyl." Accessed March 19, 2020. https://pubchem.ncbi.nlm.nih.gov/compound/indoxyl.

Wenner, Nicholas and Matthew Forkin. "Indigo: Sources, processes and possibilities." *Fibershed,* June 2017. https://fibershed.org/wp-content/uploads/2017/08/indigo-sources-processes-possibilities-june2017.pdf.

PART 5

CONCLUSION

Lee, Suzanne. "Grown your own clothes." Filmed February 2011
    at TED2011 in Long Beach, CA. Video, 06:25. https://www.ted.
    com/talks/suzanne_lee_grow_your_own_clothes/transcript.

TED. "BioDesign: The (R)evolution of Sustainable Fashion | The-
    anne Schiros | TEDxFIT." Janruary 4, 2018. Video, 17:55. https://
    www.youtube.com/watch?.

ACKNOWLEDGEMENTS

Writing a book is super challenging. Trust me, I just did it, and the only reason I got this far is because of the amazing people that supported me along the way. If it weren't for you, I would never have been able to get this far.

Thank you first and foremost to my family for supporting me in everything I do.

Thank you Eric Koester for reaching out to me on LinkedIn, and helping me start my book-writing journey.

Thank you Jem Chambers-Black, Mozelle Jordan, Brian Bies, and the entire New Degree Press publishing team. There have been many moments during this journey where I have wanted to give up, but your encouragement and support inspired me to keep going and write!

Thank you to everyone who gave me their time for a personal interview, and let me share the story of their company.

Roya Aghighi Founder of Biogarmentary

Rob Nicoll CMO and Cofounder Chip[s] Board

Nicole Ring SmartFiber Raquel Prado Sustainability and Research Maanger Ananas Anam

Karin Fleck CEO Vienna Textile Lab

Laura Luchtman Founder Living Colour

Michelle Zhu CEO of HUUE

And thank you to everyone who: pre-ordered the eBook, paperback, and multiple copies to make publishing possible, helped spread the word about *Fashion's Biofabrication Revolution* to gather amazing momentum, and helped me publish a book I am proud of. I am sincerely grateful for all your help.

Ana Shaikh	Hira Khan
Lubna Rahman	Maryam Butt
Nabil Ahmed	Salma Gill
Takwa Salem	Farrukh Ahmad
Hamid Bazaraa	Syed Haque
Fumei Jackson	Saeed Tamseel
Omer Mozaffar	Batool Siddiqui
Sana Jawaid	Sayeeda F Wahab
Sidra Hussain	Tazeen Malik
Sharjeel Haider	Fatir Abdul Haider
Lama Zaioor	Mahek Ibrahim
Wardah Mohammed	Hala Sabatto
Noerah Alvi	Quandeel Haider
Nelofer Kirmani	Maryam Khalid
Fatima Javed	Abbey Testin

Sumeed Manzoor
Manar Kashk
Khateeja Khan
Wajiha A Alikhan
Nayha Ghazali
Sajid Usmani
Afshan Kirmani
Syed Ahmed
Gayathri Menon
Sylvester Francis Alonz
Shagufta Jabeen
Asra Haque
Eric Koester
Nabila Naeem
Sabahat Adil
Yara Zaioor
Layla Khayr
Sawsan Abbadi
Mustafa Siddiqui
Yasmeen Khayr
Heba Alsheikh
Zachary Benning
Kathleen Kwenda
Robina Choudhry
Tasneem Naffakh
Nisa Syed
Seema Ahmed
Lydia Sekulovski
Khadija Kirmani
Nadia Ansari
Suzanne Quinn
Samreen Hassan

Christina Marie
Sayed Aamir
Maleeha Fatima
Shana Abraham
Kaiser Ahmad
Iqra Rehman
Sarah Abdel-Hadi
Shazia Fazili
Iqra Mustafa
Iram Ahmed
Zakirah Kamil
Harriet Medlin
Mahruq Khan
Wajiha Hyder
Rameen Awan
Yousuf Haque
Abraham Burmeister
Eliza Griffin
Atiya Kamal
Kathleen Grooms
Sarah Syed
Mohammad Habib
Nasir Haque
Maryam Haque
Iman Ahmad
Ejaz Khan
Ayaz Sheikh
Sardar Imtiaz Khan
Isabel Campbell
Sarwat Ajmal
Siraj Anwer
Naseem Shahid

Salman Muhammad
Farhan Siddiqui
Naba Wahid
Nimah Dada
Sophie Chaulk
Maelen Pantano
Nidal Arian
Dania Hanif
Irfan Khan
Seema Ahmad
Zainab Beg
Megan Geraghty

Priyanka Karwal
Khurram Ali
Ramsha Essa
Shams Zia
Fatma Ahmad
Sheema Saeed
Deema Martini
Saminah Munshi
Juveriya Ali
Samiha S Mohammed
Nabia Siddiqui
William Werblow